You Can't Talk Shit Done

You Can't Talk Shit Done

Adding Actions to Words

by
Randy Clark

Copyright © 2019 by Randy Clark
All rights reserved.

Table of Contents

Preface ix

Chapter 1: The Process 1
   When You're the Facilitator 1
   As an Attendee 11

Chapter 2: Meetings 17
   How to Get More Out of Your Meetings 17
   What Do You Do When Your Meeting Includes Remote Workers? 21
   Meetings Action Checklist 23
   It's Time to Act 25

Chapter 3: Conferences 31
   How to Get the Most Out of a Conference as an Attendee 31
   How to Engage Your Audience as a Presenter 32
   How to Be a Better Conference Networker 38

Chapter 4: Training 43
   Training Is a Process, Not a Checklist 43
   Leadership Training Isn't Osmosis 45
   Don't Ride Alone 46
   Do You Have a Management Development Plan? 48
   Are You Ready to Get Started? 49
   What Training Are Your Managers Not Getting? 51
   7 Ways to Improve Employee Engagement 54
   The Importance of Employee Engagement and Workplace Satisfaction 55
   A Workplace Engagement Checklist 56
   Cross-Training in Action 60
   Is Your Company Improving, and Will It Last? 63
   Stop Putting Off Your Business Plan 66
   Why SMART Goals Are Dumb 68
   Effective Goals Are Driven by Activities 69

Chapter 5: Presentations 75
   How to Prepare to Present 75
   3 Steps to Preparing a Killer Presentation 76
   How to Be an Engaging Presenter 78
   Adding Stories and Questions to Your Presentation 79

    Adding Action to My Fort Wayne TEDx 81
    Leadership Hendricks County 82
    Indianapolis Department of Metropolitan Development 83
    Young Business Leaders Presentation 84
    Presentations 84

Chapter 6: Seminars and Workshops 89
    A Half-Day Workshop 89
    Communicating with Customers 91

Chapter 7: Content 101
    Can a Book Take Action? 105
    Taking Action on Business Blogging 105

Chapter 8: Life 107
    Are You Waiting for Others to Change? 107
    Where Does Help Begin? 108
    Leadership Doesn't End at the Office 109
    When You Stop Learning, You Start Dying … and Your Business Does Too 110
    If You Want to Change, Change Your Lifestyle 112
    Share Your Victories 114
    Serving Others Promotes Action 115

Chapter Nine: Giving Back 119
    You Never Know When You'll Be Called to Give 119
    Who Have You Helped Today? 120
    7 Ways a Small Business Can Give Back 121
    4 Steps to Donating Your Birthday 123
    Have You Heard of Giving Tuesday? 124
    When Giving Back Comes Back 125
    Volunteering Your Way to Better Health and Wellness 127
    Conducting a Leaderless Group Exercise 130
    4 Ways Corporate Giving Helps Your Business 131
    Is Your Corporate Giving Enough? 132

A Few Last Words 133

Acknowledgements 137

About the Author 139

Table of Action Plans

Blank ACTION PLAN Form xiii
Management Style ACTION PLAN.. 5
Annual Factory Manager ACTION PLAN 7
Facilitator ACTION PLAN 9
Attendee ACTION PLAN 14
Meeting ACTION PLAN... 24
Meeting Attendee ACTION PLAN.. 27
WordCamp ACTION PLAN Handout.. 37
Networking ACTION PLAN Form... 41
Training ACTION PLAN Form.. 53
Pick Three ACTION PLAN 65
Improvement ACTION PLAN 134

Preface

In the not-too-distant future, face-to-face meetings might become a thing of the past. Seminars, conferences, and presentations might be all-digital — people will join the conversation by logging into an event, sitting at virtual tables, or milling about in holographic worlds. But they'll have much in common with the men and women from 20,000 years ago who sat around fires and shared stories, discussed the day's events, and considered the next day's duties. What they share is the human disposition to talk rather than act.

The truth is, whether past, present, or tomorrow, talk too often leads to more talk and little action.

Communication from yesterday, today, and tomorrow have this in common: Talk without action is, for the most part, ineffectual. Regardless of the medium, whether it's grunts and whistles or neural interfaces, it's only talk until something is done.

One might argue that planning, organizing, and brainstorming are forms of talk that can lead to action, and you'd be correct. But how often have any of us sat in a meeting where plans were formed and never actualized? Too often, I'm sure.

In America today, the most recognized wastes of time in the workplace are meetings. Studies and surveys have shown that most workers in the USA would rather do almost anything than attend meetings. One Harris poll[1] even showed that 17 percent of employees would rather watch paint dry than sit through a status meeting.

Why is that? Is it because meetings lack agendas, include unneeded personnel, and too often become rambling lectures? Yes, and more, but it's not only meetings — it's training sessions, conferences, symposiums, and demonstrations.

What if every meeting, instruction, and forum concluded with a plan of action? And what if that plan of action were implemented, followed up, and revised as needed? What if the participants of these sessions knew that a plan of activities was the goal of the gathering? If that were the case, would you rather watch paint dry or be part of the team creating the action plan?

The trouble is that very few business sessions end with an action plan. Most get stuck at talk. This book shows you how to get unstuck — how to elevate meetings, training sessions, and conferences past talk and into action.

You can't talk shit done. It's been tried. It doesn't work.

Throughout history, those who acted have been the ones to change the world. It's the same with your industry, your business, and even your life. Are you ready to add action to words, or do you want to talk about it some more?

Taking Action Begins Here

The key to successfully using this book — going beyond talk and adding action to words — are the *ACTION PLANS*. There are *ACTION PLANS,* checklists, and examples throughout the workbook. If you want to make meetings and training sessions effective, then you need to act. You can't *do* this book, but you can do the *ACTION PLANS.*

The *ACTION PLANS* in this book are meant as starting points. Sometimes they will fit your needs, but they won't always be exactly what you need. Please don't let that stop you from following a plan. Use what you can and then create your own.

---

[1] www.inc.com/minda-zetlin/17-percent-of-employees-would-rather-watch-paint-dry-than-attend-team-meetings.html

How many times have you read a book, gone to a seminar, or taken a class with all the good intentions of implementing what you've learned, only to find your notes six months later buried in a drawer and no action taken? Don't skip over the *ACTION PLANS*. Take the time to stop and work the plan, and you'll finish this book with a working plan of your own design.

ACTION PLAN

List the following:

Meetings you regularly participate in

_____
_____
_____

Action Taken

_____
_____
_____

Training you're involved in

_____
_____
_____

Action Taken

_____
_____
_____

Presentations, seminars, or conferences you will conduct or attend over the next 12 months

_____
_____
_____

Action Taken

_____
_____
_____
_____

Blank ACTION PLAN Form

An action plan form doesn't have to be complicated. Here's an example of a simple one:

Name _____   Date _____

Topic _____

Action Plan

_____
_____
_____
_____

Activities

_____
_____
_____
_____

Timeline (beginning date, follow-up, and completion)

_____
_____
_____
_____

Teammates involved

_____
_____
_____
_____

A Simple Plan

I use a simple plan to add action to meetings I conduct. I conclude nearly every meeting, presentation, one-on-one discussion, and training session with a plan of action, soliciting commitments from everyone involved to choose an action to take, and then, when possible, I follow up.

I said my plan was simple. It is, and if you already add action to your words, you can skip the rest of the book. However, although the plan is simple, it's hard work. It takes commitment, dedication, and fortitude. That's what I hope to share: a simple plan and the encouragement to stay the course.

How to Use This Book

I encourage you to read *You Can't Talk Shit Done* from cover to cover, and at the same time, I hope you review chapters as needed. In other words, when you're planning a meeting, go over the chapter on meetings, and if you're attending a conference, then read about conferences.

In this book, I break down adding action to words by types of interactions: meetings, presentations, seminars, conferences, training, classroom, content, giving back, and life. Although the platforms share similar types of exchanges of information, there are differences. Meetings are often a place where interactions are encouraged, which may not be the case for presentations. Seminars are more often advanced or specific training, while conferences may cover several topics under one heading with multiple presenters.

This book is also divided into two perspectives: facilitator and attendee. As a facilitator, you have the opportunity to direct others toward adding action to words, and as an attendee, you can create actions that fit your needs. Whether you're conducting a training session, consuming content, or attending a conference, there's a basic process to add action to words.

First, we'll talk about the process.

The Process

Chapter 1

Chapter 1: The Process

How many meetings, training seminars, and planning sessions have you sat through that were inundated with great ideas, only to realize later that nothing was really accomplished? And how many times have you conducted the same without creating a plan of action? Ideation is important, but what good are ideas without action?

Adding action to words begins with a thought process, a belief that talk, planning, and discussion are critical to taking action, but are only part of a process that leads to results. Talk alone isn't the process. I may be beating a dead horse, but until you completely accept that talk isn't action, nothing will change. The conference room, board room, and classroom will remain places where shit is talked about yet little is done.

When You're the Facilitator

If you're conducting a training session, giving a presentation, or facilitating a meeting, the action process begins with understanding what you want to accomplish. Start by asking yourself what action you hope to take away from your seminar. What do you want to get done? Here are a few examples:

- Strategic planning
- Identifying problems and opportunities
- Team building and motivation
- Education
- Delegating and assigning tasks
- Creating a vision

Chapter 1

- Developing a mission
- Setting goals
- Organizing
- Sharing information

These are only examples, and the purpose of your session might not be listed above, but the key is to know what you want to accomplish. Begin planning your presentation by determining what you want your audience to take away from it. What's your purpose?

Set the stage
Once you've identified your purpose, begin your presentation by setting the stage and announcing your objective.

- **Purpose:** Begin your talk by sharing your purpose, but not only in words. Use paper action sheets, PowerPoint, video, or other multimedia to appeal to multiple senses and drive your point home.
- **Goal:** Next, let your audience know that your goal is for each of them to commit to a plan of action by choosing one activity to implement. Why only one? Have you ever attended an event and taken away 20 actionable ideas? I have, and I got bogged down trying to decide where to begin. Take the attitude that one action taken is better than none begun, and keep in mind that after completing one action, others may follow.
- **Talk about the importance of taking notes:** Not only will note taking keep participants engaged, but it's also a valuable tool to help pick an action plan.

Share actionable suggestions
The focus of action ideas should stay on the purpose. Remember the goal and stay the course. Offer activity suggestions and ideas throughout the presentation.

- **List suggestions:** Before presenting, make a list of actionable takeaways on an action plan sheet to be distributed to the audience.
- **Explain how to choose an action:** Inform participants that you will share actionable ideas throughout your presentation and that they may pick any of those, combine them, or create their own.

- **Remind them:** Throughout your presentation, remind attendees of their assignment to choose one action to follow. One way I've found to effectively do this is to point out examples as I present them.

Gather actions

At the conclusion of the meeting, ask everyone for their action plan. If the size of the group permits, I like each participant to share their plan with everyone.

Follow up

At this point, a purpose has been shared, actions have been suggested, and commitments have been made. However, without follow-up, it all could come to naught. Follow-up is necessary, and it should be part of your action plan as the presenter.

- Set dates for follow-up.
- Don't wait until completion to check progress.
- Set a completion date or designate the action as ongoing.

I'm privileged to facilitate leadership development training with the management staff, team leaders, and management candidates at TKO Graphix. We meet weekly and review topics such as conflict management, silo busting, and developing checklists. I structure the meetings with group participation in mind, using open-ended questions and planned involvement. I end most seminars asking for commitments to individual action plans. Many action plans are successful, but occasionally some are forgotten, and others start well but fizzle out.

In the past when I've completed training with teammates, they've usually been direct reports. Follow-up was easy and natural because I worked with the team every day. This isn't the case with the TKO leadership training. None of the participants are my direct reports. Because of this, I missed a vital step in the training process early on: I didn't consistently follow up on the action plans.

Nancy Jarial, TKO Graphix VP of marketing, suggested we follow up on the ideas and actions we had talked about over the previous six months. I thought it was a great idea.

We identified 34 ideas and action plans that had previously been committed to, and then we met with the leadership groups and reviewed the list. Some actions had been successfully completed, and some were in process, while others had been forgotten or abandoned. Only 10 (29 percent) had been successfully implemented.

By revisiting the list, I hoped to double our success rate. We challenged the group to choose actions to champion. They did, some working in groups, others tackling the opportunities alone. The important thing was that action was being taken. For example, before the meeting, our CEO came to Nancy to discuss how to make one of the actions on the list happen. In the past, leadership had conducted facility tours with new employees, introducing them to department managers and then concluding with a Q & A session in our conference room. I volunteered to restart interdepartmental tours, showing employees how departments affect each other.

In business, talking without doing is not very productive, but unfortunately, it's widespread. But the most important lesson here was the significance of follow-up.

Make it fit — One size doesn't fit all

I recently spent an hour sharing some of my thoughts on leadership with a diverse group of business and community leaders that included CEOs, senior VPs, educators, law enforcement officials, and others. At the beginning of my time, I explained that I was going to use a shotgun approach and shoot multiple ideas at them, from basic leadership to more advanced concepts.

I explained that my goal was for each of them to pick one technique, and only one, that they would commit to implementing. Next, I passed out action plan outlines, which could be used to choose an activity to take away from the presentation.

At the end of my presentation, I went to each of them and asked what they had chosen to implement. Everyone had something they were willing to try, and many were eager to get started. Several waited to speak with me after the presentation to seek advice or share their thoughts on implementing their action plans.

My point is that even with such a diverse group, not only were individuals able to focus on taking action — they embraced the concept.

Here are two examples of action plan handouts.

Below are two action plan outlines I've used in presentations. I've included them here as examples to give you a feel for action plans. The first, the Management Style Action Plan, was used as a handout at the beginning of a meeting. Each attendee received a copy, which they began completing during the meeting.

Example One

Management Style ACTION PLAN

Take and review the *Psychology Today* Leadership Style Test at www.psychologytoday.com/us/tests/career/leadership-style-test and then choose one area to improve from the eight essentials listed below:

- Understanding team dynamics and encouraging good relationships
- Selecting and developing the right people
- Delegating effectively
- Motivating people
- Managing discipline and dealing with conflict
- Improved communicating
- Planning, making decisions, and problem solving
- Avoiding common managerial mistakes

Area of improvement
_____

Specific Challenges
_____
_____

Chapter 1

Advice and Ideas

Action Plan

Example Two

The next example is an action sheet that was passed out to a management team at the beginning of a four-day training seminar based on the *The New Manager's Workbook: A Crash Course in Effective Management*.[2] This isn't an action plan for readers to complete (unless you're working through my first book) but an example of what an action plan can be.

---

[2] Check it out at http://amzn.to/2oY2fXk.

Annual Factory Manager ACTION PLAN

Name _____

Location _____ Date _____

Communication

Choose one listening skill to improve
_____

Pick one communication improvement action
_____

Motivation

Pick one motivator to begin using with your team
_____

Improve one area of team building
_____

Fun at work

Choose one fun activity to begin at your plant
_____
_____

Time management

Pick one time-waster for self-improvement
_____

Pick one time-saver for self-improvement
_____

Chapter 1

Training

Choose a training method to begin using
_____

Meetings

Pick two of the 13 training steps to begin using immediately
_____
_____
_____

Hiring

Choose two points from the interview checklist to add to your interview
_____
_____
_____

Choose two questions from the first interview to concentrate on with every candidate
_____
_____
_____

Conflict management

Choose one technique to begin next week

- Pinch Theory
- Corrective Action Plan
- Sandwich Method

Goal setting

How will you use activities-based goal setting?

_____
_____
_____
_____
_____

Facilitator ACTION PLAN

Before facilitating a meeting or seminar, review this chapter and then use this form to plan your actions.

Name_____

Date _____

Event _____

What's your purpose for the meeting or seminar?

_____
_____
_____

What is your goal? What do you want attendees to take away?

_____
_____
_____

Chapter 1

What will you use to share your points?

- PowerPoint
- Collateral material
- Fill-in-the-blank handouts
- Video
- Other

How will you gain a commitment from attendees to take action?

_____
_____
_____
_____

How will you follow up?

_____
_____
_____

As an Attendee

As an attendee of a meeting, presentation, or conference, you might think you have little control over what you take in and, more importantly, what you take away from the event. You'd be wrong. Granted, you have almost no control over what content is shared. However, you have total control over what you focus on and your plan of action.

What's the purpose?
Before attending an event, determine its purpose. What's it about? What's to be shared? Is there collateral material about the event? Check online for reviews, ask previous attendees what they took away, and contact the presenter-facilitator for insights. Next, ask yourself if it sounds useful. Does it fit your needs?

What if you're required to attend?
Vet the meeting as if it were an optional event and look for areas of the event that might fit your needs. If it isn't what you need or doesn't seem helpful, then consider whether you should approach your management team and explain why the meeting doesn't fit your needs. Explain how your time might be better served. Caution: You don't want to step on any toes, especially your boss's. Sometimes it may be wiser to attend rather than forgo a meeting that seems unhelpful. If you do approach management about excusing yourself from the meeting, do so from the point of view of how it will benefit the team and what you could accomplish with the time.

Are there options?
Do you have choices at the event? For example, is it a conference with breakout sessions or other alternatives? If so, choose the presentations that best fit your needs. Sounds obvious doesn't it? But I for one have chosen to attend lectures based not on what best fit my needs, but rather on what sounded fun, or because I knew the presenter, or because friends invited me to join them. Your priority should always be your needs.

What do you want to take away?
Before you attend any presentation, determine what you need or want to take away from the event. Once again, it sounds like I'm stating the obvious, and I am, but that doesn't mean people do this. Most of us attend seminars and even conferences with little more than some vague idea of what we hope to gain from attending.

Chapter 1

Ask yourself:

- Where do I need help?
- What do I want to learn?
- What's best for my organization?
- What new knowledge might have the largest payback?
- What training is missing from my education or on-the-job training?
- What problems at work need immediate attention that might be helped by my attendance?
- What opportunities could be gained by new insights?

The seven questions listed above might seem redundant, and maybe they are, but by answering them, you'll have a more focused reason for attending any meeting or seminar.

Take good notes

Regardless of how good your memory is, you can't keep track of every salient point in your head. And even if you could, who would want to? Wouldn't you rather keep your mind free for creative thought?

I'm known for taking copious notes. As I take notes, I highlight the points that best fit my needs, and after the presentation, I review my notes, organizing them and once again recognizing the key takeaways.

Ask questions

Hopefully the facilitator asks for questions. When I'm speaking, I personally find it best to ask for questions throughout a presentation and then to end with a Q & A session. But what if the speaker doesn't solicit questions?

Know what you want to ask before you ask. Formulate your questions before you open your mouth. I jot questions down before I ask them.

- **Raise your hand and politely ask if you may ask a question.** The worst that could happen is the presenter refuses your request. However, it's been my experience that most speakers appreciate thoughtful questions. It shows that participants are engaged.

- **Introduce yourself to the speaker after the presentation.** Ask if they have time to answer your questions. If they don't have time, ask if you may contact them.
- **Ask the presenter for materials.** Do they have a blog, video, slides, book, case study, or white paper that may answer your questions?

Triage

Like I said, I take copious notes, and of course every single note I take is a great idea! (Not.) That's why, early in my career, I'd find six-month-old notes buried in a desk drawer with no actions taken. I had too many ideas. I was unfocused. I created decision paralysis in myself. Eventually, I learned to triage my notes. What worked best for me was to pick one action item to implement immediately, another at 30 days, and one more at 60 days. At the end of 30 days I reviewed the progress of the first action, and if it wasn't shaping up, I'd delay the second action.

Chapter 1

Attendee ACTION PLAN

Before attending an event, review this chapter and then use this form to plan your actions.

Name_____   Date_____

Event _____

What's your purpose for attending the event?
_____
_____
_____
_____

What takeaway will help you the most, and why?
_____
_____
_____
_____

Are there options such as breakout sessions and training? If so, what will you attend?
_____
_____
_____
_____

Other
_____
_____
_____
_____

The Process

Meetings

Chapter 2

Chapter 2: Meetings

I work with businesses as a consultant. One small but growing company has retained me to work with 12 managers on leadership development, one of whom, the sales manager, worked with me 20 years ago. Last week he asked me how, 20 years ago, I got so much out of him and others from our meetings. How did I conduct sales meetings that brought results? I told him. He took notes. I'll share it with you, but first let's set the stage.

How to Get More Out of Your Meetings

Have a plan
I don't care how good an extemporaneous speaker you are; you'll do better, much better, with a plan. It doesn't have to be complicated, but you should know what you want to cover, who you want to involve, and how you will deliver the message.

If you'd like to learn more about planning a meeting, read "How to Outline a Meeting" at tkographix.com/how-to-outline-a-meeting.

Follow a schedule
Set a start time, be on time, and expect others to be punctual as well. This is where most advisers tell you to have an end time as well, but I won't. You should have a "no later than" time, but not an arbitrary end time. Parkinson's Law states, "Work expands so as to fill the time available for its completion." I explain this rule before meetings and state that we may not need all the time allotted, and if that's the case, we'll end early.

Chapter 2

Don't gripe
I worked for a sales manager who conducted daily morning meetings, and every day he complained about the previous day. If business was good, he scolded the team on paperwork, and if the paperwork was good, he told us our work areas weren't professional enough. He never had a problem naming names and calling people out. After being called out in public one too many times, a team member stood up, tossed his office keys at the sales manager, and stormed out; he didn't return. A meeting isn't the place to reprimand — that should be one-on-one. A meeting is a place for recognition, not castigation.

One of the best ways to influence anyone is to recognize the good things they do. Rather than attacking their pitfalls, begin supporting their good choices. You can catch more flies with honey than with vinegar, especially during a meeting.

Avoid lecturing
Your team will only listen to 15–20 minutes of you droning on and on before they begin fading away. To avoid this, involve your team in the meeting. Give them the opportunity by asking questions rather than lecturing. Call on teammates to share, demonstrate, or offer advice. Don't be the only one in the room talking.

Don't take all day
I've conducted thousands of sales meetings. At one time, I gave meetings five days a week for more than seven years. Most of my meetings were less than 30 minutes long. The key to meeting brevity is to keep it simple by choosing one topic and not straying from it.

Eliminate distractions
Don't settle for turning phones off — leave them out of the room. Even a phone on mute is a distraction. And leave yours out of the meeting as well. Don't allow interruptions. Tell your staff to take messages and let support staff know not to disturb your meeting. Very few things in life are so urgent they can't wait 30 minutes.

Find the missing ingredient
So, what's the missing ingredient to getting the most out of every meeting? Earlier, I told the story of my former teammate asking me how I got the team to produce from meetings. The answer is all the points listed above plus *actions and commitments*. I

learned that the most effective meetings ended with an action plan and a commitment to follow through.

I begin meetings by sharing the call to action. For example, if the meeting is about reducing mistakes in paperwork, I prepare everyone to be ready to identify an action they will use to reduce paperwork errors.

Throughout the session, I offer actionable ideas. However, I always let everyone know they can devise their own action plan; they don't have to accept one of my suggestions.

As an outside leadership consultant in 2008, I facilitated a silo-busting session with leaders from several departments at TKO Graphix. I introduced the idea of choosing an action at the beginning of the meeting, gave suggestions throughout, and explained that participants could create an action other than my suggestions. One participant, Alisha, came up with the idea of highlighting a successfully completed job and then recognizing every department's contribution to its success — brilliant!

I let the team know that the action plan doesn't have to be monumental. Small steps in the right direction are still an improvement. In the example of improving paperwork, it could be as simple as running every new document through spellcheck. Not a complicated plan, but it could be effective.

Get commitments

The next step is to get a commitment from the individuals or team to take ownership of their action plans. In other words, make the activities theirs, not someone else's. I find it helpful to distribute action plan sheets that include the plan, their name, and completion dates. Next, I copy these for follow-up. I may follow up individually, or if it's a regularly scheduled meeting, I may follow up at the next meeting.

Make an action plan

The key is to pick an action and then commit to it. It's not complicated, and it works. Does it work all the time? Nope, it doesn't. But if your teammates commit to an action and stick to it even one-third of the time, that's one out of three times more than they would have without your direction. I kinda like those numbers — how about you?

The answer I gave my former teammate was that I end with an action plan and get commitments. He looked thoughtful, made a note, and said, "Yeah, that's it."

Chapter 2

I waited a minute and asked, "What's your plan?"

Meeting Outline

Date _____

Start time _____ No-longer-than time _____

1. Subject: _____

2. Suggestions for takeaways, such as activities to improve, continue, begin, or eliminate:

   _____
   _____
   _____

3. Teammates to engage: Subject, question:

   _____   _____
   _____   _____
   _____   _____

4. How this benefits the team or individual team members:

   _____
   _____
   _____

5. How to ask for a commitment to following the activities:

   _____
   _____
   _____

What Do You Do When Your Meeting Includes Remote Workers?

As I've said, before I present to a group on leadership development, whenever possible I mingle with the audience and ask what obstacles they face in the workplace. The hindrance to leadership that I hear most often is communication. From small start-ups to multibillion-dollar international corporations, it's the same chorus. The most significant hurdle most managers face is communication. Communication breakdowns happen at every level of business but are especially critical when working with remote employees. Here are a few of the keys to communicating with remote workers.

Discuss communication preferences

Not long ago, I handed out a communication preference worksheet to 10 managers. Two detached managers joined via GoToMeeting.com. The worksheet listed six forms of communication and asked each manager to rate their preference from "always" to "only with my mother." The group ranged in age from early 20s to late 40s and included eight men and two women. Their preferences varied widely.

We learned that one of the satellite managers hated email, which was significant since his district manager primarily communicated with him via email. The district manager and detached branch manager shared their individual preferences and created a communication plan to carry forward.

Set communication expectations

A sales team I worked with set the expectation for detached sales representatives to "check in" every workday morning by calling their manager to discuss their activities from the previous day. A daily calendar and to-do list, a worksheet if you will, were supposed to be sent to the manager before the conversation. However, most of the sales reps had gotten away from completing the documents. The manager ignored and excused inconsistent completion of the worksheets. He didn't share his expectations or hold his team accountable, which eventually led to a dwindling number of worksheets completed. The manager had lost control because he didn't set expectations or hold his team accountable.

Chapter 2

The manager's VP stepped in to assist and called the sales team into the office. He began by asking the team if they knew why the worksheets were required and how they could help the salespeople. Next, he held a meeting outlining the company's expectations of daily worksheets. After that, he and the manager met with each sales rep individually and asked if they had any questions or input on the worksheets and if they understood the expectations. After the meetings, the worksheets were sent daily.

Intentionally involve remote workers

It's easy to treat remote employees differently than someone working down the hall. So, what can you do to include them as part of the team?

- **Don't hold meetings without them.** Use Skype or GoToMeeting or just get them on the phone but include them in your meetings.
- **Ask for their input.** There might not be any better way to be inclusive with a remote worker than to seek their advice.
- **Keep them in the loop.** Whatever is new at the office, whether it's a new policy, training, product, or tools and materials, the detached worker needs almost everything that the office personnel receive.
- **Make some water cooler time.** Take some time to just chat with your teammates who are out of the office. Picture in your mind's eye standing together at the water cooler. What would you share?

Visit face to face

Get in your car, hop on a plane, or bring them to you, but find a way to sit down, visit, and look each other in the eye. Regardless of all the communication networks available today, nothing replaces face-to-face communication.

Listen to your remote team

Listening to your remote team isn't only about developing good listening skills; it's also about *making time to listen*.[3] Business moves fast, and too often we rush through activities so we can mark another thing off our to-do list. Don't let making time to listen to your offsite direct reports become one of those rushed activities.

Improving communication with remote workers begins with you

---

[3] tkographix.com/how-to-actively-listen-in-a-loud-world/

In some ways, communication with remote workers today is easier than it was 20 years ago, and in other ways it's more difficult. We have more than beepers, landlines, and fax machines today, but because we have so many communication options, it can become confusing. If you discuss preferences, set expectations, and spend time with your teammates, you'll improve communication, and that's where most improvement begins.

Meetings Action Checklist

Begin meetings with an action goal. Let the attendees know your goal of choosing action plans and committing to them.

Share ideas. Give examples of actions, and then allow each person to choose one or create their own.

End meetings with a call to action. Most meetings should conclude with an action plan and commitment.

Write it down. Note the actions each has committed to and be ready to review them.

Follow up. Don't wait until the next meeting and then embarrass attendees because they forgot the action they planned to take. Check between meetings. Send an email or stop for a quick chat to remind them of their commitment.

Review the action. Begin the next meeting by asking what was learned. Let each person share their story.

Are you ready for some action? If so, here's your action plan:

Chapter 2

Meeting ACTION PLAN

Your next meeting, presentation, or training topic is
_____

5 suggested actions for the team

_____
_____
_____
_____
_____
_____
_____
_____

List each team member's action commitment

_____
_____
_____
_____
_____
_____
_____
_____
_____
_____
_____
_____
_____
_____
_____

Set a time to follow up
___

Review the action plans
___
___
___
___
___
___
___
___
___
___
___
___

It's Time to Act

So far, I've talked about how to add action to your words in meetings from the meeting leader's point of view, but what if you're not in control? What if you're a participant? How can you add action when you're not the one leading the meeting?

Too much time is wasted in meetings. According to a study by Wrike,[4] an online collaboration and project management company, "Today's office professionals not only hate meetings — 46 percent think at least some of the meetings they attend are a waste of time." Have you sat through meetings where you'd rather be anywhere else? I have,

---
[4] www.inc.com/minda-zetlin/its-official-half-your-meetings-are-a-waste-of-time-.html

Chapter 2

but over the last few years, I've worked at eliminating meetings from my schedule that don't help me reach my goals. So, that's the first step.

You might be thinking, "Well, that's nice, but I have meetings I'm required to attend that I'm not gaining much from." If that's the case — if you're required to attend — then why not take charge of your involvement and focus on actions you *can* take from the meeting?

Learn what's to be covered in the meeting. Ask for the topic of the meeting and, a few days before the meeting is scheduled, connect the dots by analyzing how the topic relates to your department, job, and goals. It might be easy to conclude, or prove, that it doesn't fit your situation, but if you look closely, there's almost always a connection. It may be indirect — for example, if the topic is focused on something from another department, it could be that by considering how the topic affects the other department, you learn how it impacts you and your department.

I once attended a meeting about paperwork mistakes directed at a company's customer service department. Members of other departments were called to the meeting primarily to share examples of continued mistakes made by the customer service reps. Most of the other department managers contributed only by sharing the mistakes made by the offending team. However, one production manager took it further. He asked what he could do to help reduce mistakes. He was told to bring every mistake to the department manager's attention. It seems the head of customer service wasn't aware of all the mistakes. Too often other departments merely complained about problems but didn't act to improve them or inform the customer service manager. The production manager began documenting every mistake and bringing it to the customer service manager. Eventually, the production manager was told to take mistakes directly to the customer service reps and to CC the manager on the communication.

Mistakes weren't completely eliminated, but the production manager's continued effort led to a reduction in mistakes. He never gave up. He had added action to the meeting — an action that directly affected his department's efficiency.

Although he had chosen an action outside of his control, he looked for a way make it better. When he brought mistakes to the customer service team's attention, he did so without being acrimonious or accusatory. He wasn't there to belittle anyone. He was there to help. A year later, he was dealing with far fewer mistakes, his job was easier, and his department's production increased.

And you can do the same. This approach shouldn't be limited to meetings, but also used with presentations, seminars, and training. Be the exception by putting your words into action. You can start today.

Meeting Attendee ACTION PLAN

Meeting topic

_____
_____
_____
_____
_____

Possible Actions

_____
_____
_____
_____
_____
_____
_____

Action Commitment — What takeaway are you committing to act on?

_____
_____
_____

Chapter 2

First action — How will you begin your action?

_____
_____
_____
_____
_____

Follow-up

_____
_____
_____
_____
_____
_____
_____
_____
_____
_____

Meetings

Conferences

Chapter 3

Chapter 3: Conferences

I've talked with scores of conference attendees before, during, and after gatherings and repeatedly heard the same two questions: "I've got so many ideas and takeaways from the conference, where do I start?" and "How can I become better at networking?" On the other side of the coin, I've sat with presenters as we discussed how to better connect with our audiences.

In this chapter, I share thoughts on all three: How to get the most out of a conference as an attendee, how to engage your audience as a presenter, and how to be a better conference networker.

How to Get the Most Out of a Conference as an Attendee

First, have a plan
At most conferences, you'll be bombarded with information. There'll be keynote speakers and breakout presenters, work sessions with industry leaders, and opportunities to connect with old friends and new. But what are the takeaways? Do they fit your needs? The question becomes — is it worth the time and money? If it's a legitimate event, it's up to you to make it effective.

Attending any event without a plan will most certainly ensure wasted time and money. If you don't have a plan, stay home. A plan doesn't have to be complicated or take days to prepare. It begins with knowing what you hope to gain. Are you looking for specific ideas, inspiration, or how to improve your operation? One way to accomplish this is to form a discussion panel.

Form a discussion panel
Forming a discussion panel is easy to do if you're attending with co-workers or friends. It's a little more difficult when you're alone. If you're going by yourself, reach out via social media for three or four others to join a discussion panel. The panel should meet for a few minutes at lunch or after sessions to discuss and share.

If there are breakouts, use panel members to cover every session possible. Share notes, ideas, and thoughts about each session. Assign each member to bring one takeaway from each session. It's important to limit the number of ideas shared or the discussion may bog down.

Chose three actions
During the last panel discussion, each member should choose three actions to implement. Only three? Doesn't sound like enough? It might not be. You might have a great capacity, but then again, at previous events, you may have been a "slacktivist" with a pad full of notes you did little with. If that's the case, try three actions. Begin the first immediately, the second in 30 days, and the third in 90 days (giving time for one and two to get rolling).

Each panel member should share their three actions with the group with the idea of holding each other accountable. Next, schedule follow-ups by email, social media, or at the coffee shop. Finally, encourage continuing interaction among panel members.

How to Engage Your Audience as a Presenter

3 Easy Ways to Engage Your Audience
TKO Graphix sponsored the Master of Business Online[5] conference. Once again it was an outstanding event — I left with actionable ideas. Before his presentation, Chad Pollitt[6] asked me to critique his presentation, "Embracing Digital Personas."[7] It was thought-

---

[5] www.getyourmbo.com
[6] twitter.com/ChadPollitt
[7] www.slideshare.net/cpollittiu/embracing-digital-personas

provoking, entertaining, and filled with takeaways ... so there wasn't a lot to critique. I did, however, share three audience involvement strategies that have helped me.

How to involve your audience

1. **Arrive early and mix with the crowd.** Introduce yourself and ask what attracted them to your session and what they hope to gain from the presentation. Ask specific questions that you know will be pertinent to your presentation, and if their answer fits, ask if you may call on them during your talk. Identifying several people to call on paves the way for others to feel comfortable participating and will add another level of engagement to your presentation.
2. **Ask open-ended questions throughout your presentation.** Don't settle for closed, leading questions, like "You know what I mean, don't you?" Ask the audience what, why, and how.
3. **At the end of your presentation, after Q & A, ask the audience what they got out of the presentation.** Set it up by asking the group to think about one takeaway from your presentation they will embrace. Then ask the group in general and call on specific individuals to share what they learned and how they plan to use it.

There are many ways to involve your audience in a presentation. You can give assignments, hand out action sheets to complete, send follow-up information via email, or post a social media call to action. All these strategies can help you connect with your audience. By being proactive, you can affect how your audience engages with you and not leave it up to chance. So, let me ask you — what's your takeaway from this section of the book?

3 Examples of Audience Participation in Action
1. Down on the Farm
One day last summer, while checking my CreateSpace account, I noticed that a large number of my first book had been ordered that week. This had happened before, and I always wondered who purchased the books. Amazon and CreateSpace don't share buyer information. I know that companies large and small have purchased *The New Manager's Workbook: A Crash Course in Effective Management*[8] and use it as the basis for management development programs, but I rarely know which companies are interested.

---

[8] www.amazon.com/New-Managers-Workbook-Effective-Management-ebook/dp/B01BUKOUVI

Chapter 3

However, this time I learned who the buyer was. The organization, Indiana Farm Bureau Insurance, reached out to me, told me they had bought my book, and asked if I would present at a weekend conference for supervisors. I was delighted to participate.

I was allotted one hour for my presentation. There were more than 40 attendees. I began by introducing myself and explaining my role as facilitator; then I shared my goal, which was to have everyone in the room pick one action to commit to implementing within their district. Next, I handed out worksheets, which were more of an action plan. They could use the sheets to note ideas throughout my presentation as well as identify actions.

I saved 15 minutes at the end of the presentation and went around the room asking everyone to share their commitment. Everyone had chosen, most sounded enthusiastic about their choice, and some even choose two! (I had great fun with those who choose two, calling them rule breakers!) The bottom line is that I'm convinced that a large percentage of the managers left my presentation with an action plan of their own, one that spoke to them.

2. WHEN THE AUDIENCE RAN THE SHOW

A few years ago, I presented at Blog Indiana, a forum that, unfortunately, no longer exists. It was a great place to meet other like-minded bloggers, social media marketers, content developers, and more. For my third-year presenting, I decided to do something different. Unlike my previous talks, I decided not to discuss social media or blogging, but to talk about helping each other.

I belong to a brainstorming/networking group called Friend Up. We meet the first Saturday and third Thursday of every month and have a private group on Facebook. At that third Blog Indiana conference, my friend Allison Carter and I shared a brief outline of how our Friend Up group worked. We handed out numbered worksheets with a list of questions, and then asked everyone with an odd-numbered sheet to change tables (something Allison and I had used successfully to mix up the group of attendees at previous presentations). The questions included

- What did you hope to gain from attending this presentation?
- How can I help you?
- What industry, organization, or person would you like to be introduced to?

We had 45 minutes scheduled for the presentation, 30 of which was spent letting the people at each table connect. When time was up, I had to stop the conversations. They were engaged. Andy Hollandbeck, a future Friend Upper, told me after the session that he'd never been to a presentation where the audience did all the work.

Only a couple of weeks ago, my good friends Paul and Naomi D'Andrea joined my wife Cathi and me for dinner, and the topic of how long we'd known each other came up. I had forgotten that Paul had attended that presentation. That day, he met me and others whom he continuess to connect with eight years later. We didn't just try to talk shit done — we did it.

3. Lessons from WordCamp Cincinnati
According to WordCamp Central,[9] "WordCamp is a conference that focuses on everything WordPress. WordCamps are informal, community-organized events that are put together by WordPress users like you. Everyone from casual users to core developers participate, share ideas, and get to know each other."

My point of view at WordCamp Cincinnati was from two perspectives — as an attendee and as a presenter. Both views were outstanding. I enjoyed the breakout presentations, learned a lot, and was pleasantly surprised by the engagement and participation of the audience during my presentation.

Skip a session and connect
Nearly everyone I talked to was open to conversation, sharing their knowledge, and willing to help. I made a few connections that I expect will continue long after WordCamp. During the opening remarks, Aaron Forgue suggested everyone skip one session and conduct a "hallway session," networking with others.

It didn't matter how people used WordPress, whether it was for a company store, a blogging platform, or an agency that built business websites, everyone was hungry to learn, willing to share, and ready to connect. My kind of peeps.

A successful event must be well-planned and organized
This was my first WordCamp, and maybe this team was more organized than others, but I doubt it. WordCamps have been going on long enough to be systemized, and WordCamp

---

[9] https://central.wordcamp.org

Chapter 3

Cincinnati ran like clockwork. The organizers and volunteers did an outstanding job. I was amazed at how much they accomplished with such a low admission fee. There was a spirit of cooperation that rivaled any event I'd ever attended. The staff was there to help, and they did — not only the staff, but the organizers and other attendees were helpful as well. Here's an example:

Friday before the event, there was a reception for speakers and volunteers. At the reception, I mentioned the soon-to-be-released WordPress editor Gutenberg and was immediately directed to Andrew Duthie, who not only was the event organizer but also helped develop Gutenberg. Andrew answered my questions and shared about the new editor for more than 20 minutes. Thank you, Andrew!

Be available to help
I spent a lot of time in WordPress 101, where Dustin Hartzier and Brian Retterer did a masterful job of going over WordPress basics and answering questions from multiple levels of participants.

Earlier I mentioned how accessible and accommodating everyone was. I want to share an example that defined WordCamp for me and blew me away. Saturday afternoon, I ran into Brian Retterer again. I told him I had missed one section of his presentation, and he immediately pulled out his laptop, set it on a nearby counter, and shared the content I had missed. Wow. Just wow. For me, that epitomized WordCamp: good people wanting to learn, help, and share. They did more than talk.

My presentation at WordCamp
My presentation was based on my book *How to Stay Ahead of Your Business Blog Forever*.[10] I began the presentation by distributing the action sheet below. Next, I shared my goal that everyone in attendance get at least one idea from the presentation that they would commit to act upon. I covered how to identify topics that fit one's brand, coming up with post ideas, editing actions, and SEO basics. I include the handout here as an example of a convention presentation handout.

---

[10] Find it online at https://amzn.to/2GwDnRX.

WordCamp ACTION PLAN Handout

Action: Identify Four Blog Categories

1. _____
2. _____
3. _____
4. _____

Action: List Four Blog Post Ideas

1. _____
2. _____
3. _____
4. _____

Action: Readability — Pick one

- Flesch Reading Ease Score
- Number of Words Following a Subhead
- Size of Paragraphs
- Length of Sentences
- Transition Words
- Sentence Structure

Chapter 3

> Action: SEO — Pick One
>
> - Meta Description
> - Slug
> - Keyword in Title
> - Keyword in the First Paragraph
> - Keyword Density
> - Number of Words
> - Alt Text
> - Cornerstone Content

After my presentation
At the end of my presentation, I told the audience I'd be in the common area to answer any questions. I had mentioned my book on blogging during the presentation, and several asked if I had any copies with me for sale. I had five copies, which I gave away. The after-presentation discussion convinced me that people were doing more than talking about blogging — they'd made action plans.

How to Be a Better Conference Networker

As I said at the beginning of this chapter, one common complaint or self-critique I often hear at conferences is the lack of networking acumen. I believe most of us make networking too difficult by building high expectations with no plan, no ladder to reach those heights. Good networking isn't based on charisma, it's not the domain of extroverts alone, and you don't have to be the smartest person in the room. An effective networker has a plan.

How about *we* make a plan — what do you say?

Don't just talk with folks at conferences — connect and help
Whom should you target to connect with? It ties back to what you want to achieve. I'm a firm believer that you never know how any two people might help each other until you ask. Start by looking at the speaker lineup, choose one or two speakers you'd like to meet, attend their sessions, and then introduce yourself. I promise they will not bite. Next, review the attendees and, once again, pick a few people you want to meet and go introduce yourself.

I'm going to make this easy
Before you tell me you're too shy, you don't know what to say, and you don't want to impose, try this. Instead of introducing yourself with some awkward version of an elevator pitch, ask them a question.

"Hi, I'm Randy. I enjoyed your presentation about butterflies. How did you come up with that?"

"Hi, my name's Randy Clark. I saw you were attending and wanted to meet you. May I ask why you chose to attend this event, what you hope to get out of it, and how I can help?"

"Hi, my name's John Doe, and I read this book where this guy said I should introduce myself to others and ask how I could help them. So, what are you hoping to gain from this event and how can I help you?"

Don't make it complicated. Keep it simple. Introduce yourself and ask how you can help.

The new networking is connecting people
Maybe it shouldn't be called *networking*. Maybe it should be called *connect-working*. Connections can be made at networking events, but networking isn't connecting. The best networking strategy is to be helpful, and one of the most helpful things anyone can do is to connect people who can help each other.

People want to connect.

Earlier, I discussed Friend Up[11], the organic help network I'm a member of. A couple of years ago, Allison Carter[12] and I traveled the state presenting to social media clubs about

---
[11] Learn more about FriendUps at http://tkographix.com/creating-networking-group-rocks.
[12] www.linkedin.com/in/allisonlcarter

connecting. As we had at Blog Indiana, at the beginning of the presentation we distributed numbered worksheets and then, near the end, asked all the odd-numbered attendees to switch seats. That got folks sitting with people they didn't know. When they were settled in, we asked everyone to turn to someone near them and ask, "What brought you here today and how can I help you?" We followed up by asking everyone to ask a neighbor the following: "What individual, organization, or industry would you like to be introduced to?" We always had to interrupt the conversation to finish our presentation — people wanted to share, they wanted to help each other.

HOW TO CONNECT PEOPLE
Connecting people starts by serving others and not yourself. Caring about others is the key to connecting people to one another.

- Ask people where they need help and how you might assist.

- Learn what connections others desire. Whom do they want to meet and why?

- Look for connections others might not see. Not every connection is obvious, and even obvious connections can go unnoticed.

WHY CONNECT PEOPLE?
Connecting people leads to expanded friendships and more meaningful relationships, but for me, making a connection is a reward in itself. I understand that may not be true for everyone, so here's a reason you can take to the bank: Connecting people never feels sleazy, like overt promotion of personal interest often does. Connecting people builds a network of friends that can be called upon to offer advice, support initiatives, and promote calls to action. Connecting people connects you.

Commit to connect-working
I want you to make a commitment at your next networking opportunity to connect two people. It may be friends who have never met, or they may have met and never realized how they could help each other. Two people, one connection — that's all. Of course, after you've done it once …

Conferences

Networking ACTION PLAN Form

Whom do you want to meet?

_____
_____
_____

What do you need?

_____
_____
_____
_____

How will you introduce yourself?

_____
_____
_____

How can you help?

_____
_____
_____
_____

Who could you connect to another?

_____
_____
_____

Training

Chapter 4

Chapter 4: Training

Training Is a Process, Not a Checklist

I was talking with a group of managers last week about conflict resolution when the topic of corrective action came up. We discussed when corrective action should be taken or, more accurately, when it shouldn't be considered. When a team or individual doesn't deliver the expected activity or results, a manager should determine the causes before jumping to disciplinary action or critiques. The leader should determine whether there were outside consequences that affected the result, whether the teammates involved have the tools they needed, and if were they properly trained. Because if they weren't trained — they don't need discipline, they need training.

So, what is proper training? It means that trainees have the knowledge and skills to follow the training. They know what to do, how to do it, and why to do it that way. It doesn't mean they were shown once and then handed a checklist.

An installation manager I worked with would hire inexperienced people of character and then train the installation position. He onboarded by distributing a manual to trainees before training began. During training, he gave them a checklist and then showed them each step in the process. After he completed a step, he watched as each trainee completed each step. Next, he assigned tasks and left, but checked progress throughout the task. Before a trainee "graduated," they took an open-book test using the manual he

Chapter 4

had given them. Before any new installer was sent to a jobsite, the manager knew they had the skills to complete the job.

The manager also gave the trainees expectations throughout the training, which continued when they went on the job. He didn't talk training done — he acted.

A few years ago, I took over the sales training for one of the top 50 home remodelers in America. Their recruiting and hiring processes were good, and from what I saw they hired people who should be able to do the job.

They had an intense and thorough training program. New hires began on a Monday and spent six to eight hours each day in the classroom, after which they rode with a tenured salesperson on appointments, observing practical application of what they'd seen in the classroom. After working until 8 or 9 p.m., they had assignments to complete. After all that, they were expected to go by themselves to an appointment on their sixth day — Saturday — and make a sell.

The problem was, the new salespeople didn't sell. Often, it was weeks before their first sale, which was expensive for the company and discouraging to the salespeople.

I spent a week observing the training, reviewing their literature, and interacting with a class of new salespeople and then took charge of the following class.

I made only one substantial change to the organization's training plan: I set expectations from the beginning and tied every piece of training to that expectation. In that first class, I told the trainees they were all expected to sell on Saturday, their first day on their own. I continued by explaining I would do my part and give them everything they needed to make this happen. Next, I explained that this would only work if they worked. If they followed my instructions, learned the material, and completed their assignments, they would be successful.

Throughout the training, I tied every step of the training to the expectation of selling on their first day. For example, part of the presentation was sharing the company's history, which was impressive. The business had won numerous awards for quality work and customer service, which inspired trust from prospects, but only if it was presented well. When I gave the assignment of learning the company story, I reiterated how important this assignment was to achieve their first sell. To add to that, I explained that each trainee would be videotaped presenting the company story in role play so they could critique their own performance.

With that one change — sharing expectations — the first-day sell for new salespersons went from almost zero to more than 90 percent.

Okay, so you don't train salespeople. It doesn't matter. Whatever and whoever you train can be enhanced by setting clear expectations and then tying training to those expectations.

Leadership Training Isn't Osmosis

I do a lot of leadership training. I'm currently conducting nine leadership development classes for three organizations at varying levels of management, from management trainees to departmental managers. Those are my regular weekly and biweekly classes. I also present and conduct meetings on leadership development for organizations, businesses, and the government. I'm often asked, "What training do you recommend for managers?"

What training do managers need?
Managers need leadership training, which covers all the activities they're responsible for, especially when it comes to managing people.

What doesn't work is being thrown into the deep end
When I was a new manager, one of my first tasks was to hire additional personnel. I was told to place an ad, answer phone calls, interview candidates, and hire three people. That's all the instruction I received.

I don't need to go into detail, but I wasn't very successful at hiring. You might have similar stories, maybe not with hiring, but with conducting a meeting, completing a corrective action, or supervising new hire training. Regardless, too many managers, especially new frontline managers, are thrown into the deep end — sink or swim.

What managers need are systems and procedures, not only covering what to do, but how to do it, and why it's important. For example, as a new manager, when I was asked to hire three people, telling me to do it wasn't enough; I needed to know how. Knowing what ads had been successful, outlining a script for answering ad calls, and having interview questions would have been a good start. However, that should only have been the beginning. To be competent at hiring, I needed training. I needed to know what systems to use, how to complete them, and why to use them.

What will your managers be asked to do?
Whatever responsibilities are given to frontline managers, they need more than being told what to do. If they're expected to conduct meetings, train, and complete corrective actions, then they need the tools to do so — the what, how, and why. Here are a few of the most common tasks frontline managers are expected to complete:

- Recruit and hire
- Train
- Conduct meetings
- Motivate and team build
- Complete employee reviews
- Communicate with staff and other departments
- Manage conflict
- Solve problems
- Manage schedules

Your managers might not do all of these, and they may have other responsibilities. But regardless of the task, if you want frontline managers to have the best chance at success, you need to supply the training they need.

Don't Ride Alone

When I was a sales manager for one of the top remodelers in America, I ran appointments six days a week, two or three on weekdays and one or two on Saturday. I was in the position for several years. I never went to an appointment alone; I always had a sales representative with me. It was not only part of my training system; it was the most important cog in the wheel. I never rode alone.

Get to know your teammates
I used my time riding with sales representatives to get to know them better. I learned about their passions, their desires, and what they wanted out of the job. You might not

have alone time on a drive to an appointment, but you can take the same approach. Invest time finding out what motivates your teammates.

Ride with new people
I would ride with new sales representatives and show them the live-action version of what I taught in the classroom. You're probably not on sales calls with new employees, but you can do the same thing: Take what they've been trained and show them how it's done. It doesn't have to be you; it can be, but it can also be any competent teammate who follows procedure.

Don't forget your experienced people
Sometimes I would take an experienced teammate with me on an appointment and then sit back and watch. I always found at least one action I could compliment, and one area we could improve. Do the same thing with your team: Sit back and watch what they do. I guarantee you'll find something to compliment and an opportunity for improvement.

Train the next person up
Occasionally, I'd take assistant managers and leadership development trainees with me. During our time together, I'd ask their advice and opinions about our team. I'd involve them in the planning process and mentor them on leadership best practices. You can do the same, whether it's over lunch, on the way to a seminar, or during planned one-on-one time.

Make your job easier
Besides never riding alone on sales calls, I'd bring teammates with me on projects. At one time, I supervised the installation department at the remodeling company. I had people shadow me when we implemented a new vendor check-in system, sit with me during employee critiques, and shadow me on installation inspections. Eventually, I turned all those activities over to others. I'd trained them how to do it. I didn't ride alone.

Train your replacement
If you want to progress, you have to have someone who can fill your shoes. The next time you think about managing a project alone, stop and ask yourself whether this is a training opportunity and, if so, who should ride with you.

Chapter 4

Do You Have a Management Development Plan?

Currently, at TKO Graphix, I facilitate six management development training classes. Two groups meet every week for 30 to 45 minutes, and the other four meet every other week. Why does TKO Graphix do this? Because as good as their current management team is, they want to be even better. They want to go from good to great, as well as develop future leaders. What plan does your organization have to develop and improve your leadership team?

Does your organization have a management development plan, or do you throw new managers into the deep end hoping they keep their head above water? If the latter is your system — how's it working so far?

Time after time I hear stories about organizations scrambling to find the next manager because the current leader gave two days' notice ... an hour ago. I hear stories about micro-managers, bullies who use intimidation as a motivator, do-as-I-say-not-as-I-do bosses, and more. I hear about the difficulty in keeping remote management teams all on the same page. When I hear this, I share that I have an answer. It's not easy, and it's not perfect, but it's a darn good start. It's a management development program that anyone can do.

You and your team can improve the consistency of your managers, recognize and prepare your next managers, and teach best practices to your management staff.

Why conduct management training?
There are many reasons to offer management and leadership training.

- Establishes consistent management practices throughout the company.
- Shows interest in employees, which leads to improved job satisfaction and increased performance.
- Develops camaraderie among teammates from different departments and busts silos.
- Provides a management forum to share information and ideas.
- Trains the best practices to achieve the highest results directly affecting the bottom line.

How can management development be conducted?
- **Current managers:** Meet monthly, or more frequently as needed, for 30- to 45-minute training sessions.
- **Remote managers:** Options include centrally located group meetings, online participation through apps like Skype, or prerecorded sessions.
- **Future managers:** Have direct managers recognize and nominate candidates. Create a management candidate profile and survey to determine whether the individual fits management expectations. Conduct 30- to 45-minute leadership training sessions monthly, or more frequently as needed, with all management candidates.

Are You Ready to Get Started?

I'm passionate about management development. Can you tell? Below, I've listed two of my books on leadership training. I and others recommend them as the basis for a management training program. They can be purchased on Amazon or Barnes and Noble, but that's not important to me. What matters to me is getting the word out and offering managers the help and guidance they need. What I and others didn't receive. So, if you're not in a position to purchase the book, contact me, and I'll give you a copy because what's important is helping people, not how many books I sell.

Ready, set, go — what are you waiting for? Are you waiting for the next time you're stuck with no manager, or when you find out your West Coast district manager hasn't conducted reviews, or when you see a manager critiquing an employee in front of the team? Yes, you could wait until you're desperate, or you could start now. The workbook *The New Manager's Workbook: A Crash Course in Effective Management* is available on Amazon at www.amazon.com/New-Managers-Workbook-Effective-Management-ebook/dp/B01BUKOUVI.

For more advanced training, try *The Manager's Guide to Becoming a Leader* available at www.amazon.com/Managers-Guide-Becoming-Leader/dp/1984951289.

But don't take my word for it
Here are a few reviews of the workbook:

Chapter 4

> I consider myself a scholar in leadership theory and practice and have enjoyed the academic journey. I have also read countless leadership books written by greats like Collins, Sinek, Maxwell, and others. ... I came across Randy Clark's *New Manager's Workbook*. When I read the material, I realized how brilliantly put together his book was! I have made this tool available for the company's new managers with great reviews. This is very much a "crash course" that is perfect for that person who gets thrown into a management role and wants to find early success.

> Our business bought copies for every manager and we're using it in leadership training classes. I was one of the first in our organization to embrace his leadership methods, and it changed how I managed people. I had never looked at managing as helping people, but it works, and I am a better manager because of it. Managing people doesn't have to be confrontational. It's a commonsense approach to leadership that can be used in the office and at home.

> I have been in management for 20+ years but never truly had a grasp on being a manager. It is not just being in charge! This book has given me a path to becoming a more effective manager and what it means to manage people and the activities to make them more successful! This book is a must-read for anyone involved in management.

If this is the training you're looking for, if it's what's missing from your organization, contact me at randyclarkleadership.com#contact. I love talking about leadership training, and hopefully I can offer some constructive advice.

A phone call from a professor

I received a phone call from Juergen Kneifel, a member of the faculty at Everett Community College. He's using my *New Manager's Workbook* to teach a business course called "The Fundaments of Supervision." He was looking for a book that would prepare future businesspeople for the day-to-day challenges they'd face. He shared with me that when he completed his bachelor's and took a position in business management, he was unprepared. School had taught him business theory but not practical management activities. I told him it was the same when I was a new manager. We both believe this is true for many.

What Training Are Your Managers Not Getting?

What's missing from the toolbox your frontline managers need to successfully drive your business? Stop and ask yourself what responsibilities they have. Do they have the tools — the policies, procedures, guidelines, checklists, and training — to accomplish what they're responsible for? Are your frontline managers put in a position to succeed or to fail?

One of the businesses where I facilitate leadership training retained me to work with two levels of managers, experienced department-level managers and new managers and management candidates. Working with the group of experienced managers has been rewarding and fun. Heck, they teach me almost as much as I share with them. The material I share with the first group fits three categories: activities they know and use, things they used to do and got away from, and new management techniques.

However, working with new managers and management trainees is different. Much of what we discuss is new to them. To watch someone, stop, gaze thoughtfully, and then take a note or highlight a section of their book is rewarding. To hear them discuss using what they've learned always puts a smile on my face. And whenever I see these young people "getting it," I think back to when I and others — like professor Kneifel — were new managers. This is what was missing from our management training. I'm sure I can speak for Mr. Kneifel when I say that our experience of being thrown into the deep end is a big part of why we're passionate about management and leadership development today.

One way to assess your management development leadership training and give your team the training it needs and wants is to conduct a survey. Here's an example.

Chapter 4

Training Survey

Trainee Name _____ Date _____

1. What key concept did you take from the training?
_____
_____

2. Was the topic relevant, and is it information you will use?
_____
_____

3. What was the purpose of the training?
_____
_____

4. What would you have discussed further?
_____
_____

5. What could have been improved?
_____
_____

6. What topics would you like to explore in the future?
_____
_____

7. What are your assignments?
_____
_____

8. What commitments have you made regarding using the training?
_____
_____

Before you begin a training session, take a few minutes and consider what you want to accomplish. What key points do you want your trainees to take away? How will you present the key points, and how will you gain a commitment from the students to follow through with a commitment to use the training? The following action plan might help organize your training plan.

Training ACTION PLAN Form

Introduce today's topic. List what will be covered and why.

_____
_____
_____
_____
_____
_____

Make note of the previous training session for review; consider giving a quiz.

_____
_____
_____
_____

Share today's objective (what you want to accomplish and why) as well as the expectations of the day.

_____
_____
_____
_____

Close with commitments from attendees, reminder of your expectations for them, and, if appropriate, preparation for next quiz.

Chapter 4

7 Ways to Improve Employee Engagement

Multiple studies have shown that engaging employees reduces turnover, absenteeism, and tardiness. Engaged employees take more pride in their work, and people who take pride in their work are happier and healthier. Engaged and invested employees become evangelists for their organizations, sharing their pride with family, friends, and customers. Do you need another reason to improve employee engagement? Engaged teammates affect the bottom line. According to a 2013 Gallup meta-analysis[13] of 1.4 million employees, organizations with a high level of engagement report 22 percent higher productivity.

Is it time to improve employee engagement in your workplace? Here's how.

Hire the right people. Employees who are a bad fit will be difficult, if not impossible, to assimilate into the work culture. Too often, organizations hire primarily for skill without considering fit. We've all worked with a teammate who had talent and skill but didn't fit the culture or made poor character choices. Hire for character, cultural fit, and skills.

Train, and then train some more. Training should begin the first day of an employee's career, but it shouldn't end after basic training. When an organization offers follow-up training, continuous improvement seminars, and leadership development, it shows employees that it cares about them. People want to know someone cares.

Share a vision. People want to know the work they do matters, and they want to know how their efforts affect the whole. Last year, while visiting my father in the hospital, I chatted with a housekeeper. I asked her about her job, and she explained at length how important following her checklist to the best of her ability was for patients and staff. She was part of the vision. She was engaged.

Listen and respond. Everyone wants a boss they can talk to, but it doesn't end there. People want a boss who gives them answers, even if it's not always what they hope to hear. Teammates want feedback. They don't want to be ignored or lied to and lying by omission is still a lie. The truth is engaging.

---

[13] www.gallup.com/workplace/236927/employee-engagement-drives-growth.aspx

Involve the team. Ask for input and ideas. The people doing the work might know more about what they need than the bosses do. Conduct a survey and ask for suggestions to improve the company, product, and work environment. Even if their ideas and input aren't used, people become more engaged when they're asked for their opinions.

Recognize performance, milestones, and character. When an employee has been a loyal contributor for a year, five, or ten, celebrate it. When teammates show good character, such as dependability, relish it, and when folks do outstanding work, recognize them. Need some ideas on how to recognize employees? Read "101 Super Effective Ways to Reward Your Employees" [14] by Peter Economy at Inc.com.

Say thank you. Recognize an employee or team of the month. Tell people you appreciate their work. Thank someone for their effort, for going above and beyond, or for doing excellent work. A simple thank you can go a long way. Employees who feel appreciated are engaged employees.

The Importance of Employee Engagement and Workplace Satisfaction

Employee engagement and workplace satisfaction may be the most significant keys to employee retention, consistent top-notch performance, and increased production. Although most organizations know and understand this, few follow through with the activities it takes to create an engaged company culture of satisfied employees. Some managers give lip service to the importance of workplace satisfaction, others deny the need for employee engagement, and many underestimate the significance of employee engagement to job satisfaction.

What does your business care about?
Engaged employees are more satisfied with their work, and happy employees accomplish more. An employee who believes an organization has their best interest in mind is generally willing to do more for the business. When a business cares about its employees, employees care about the business.

---

[14] www.inc.com/peter-economy/101-super-effective-ways-to-reward-your-employees.html

Chapter 4

Disengaged employees are not the most productive. They don't willingly take on more or go above and beyond. Quite often they couldn't care less about quality, deadlines, or following procedures. When a company doesn't honor their employees, the employees don't honor the company.

Increased engagement = job satisfaction = higher performance
It's not complicated. Engaging employees leads to increased job satisfaction, which in turn lowers employee turnover and improves productivity. So how can an organization engage employees? Here are 15 ideas. Some of these ideas engage teammates directly, others are more indirect, but all are impactful.

A Workplace Engagement Checklist

Where does your workplace rank as far as employee engagement and satisfaction? Score what your business offers. From a high of 10 down to 0.

10 always, 5 sometimes, 0 never. (Use all numbers 0 through 10)

___Continuous training

___ Daily feedback

___Wellness initiatives

___Luncheons and pitch-ins

___Employee surveys

___Group participation in charitable events

___Flexible scheduling

___Rewards for increased production

___Recognition for achievement, milestones, and character

___Open-door, transparent management

___Company outings

___Memberships, such as gyms and fitness clubs

___Dress-up, casual, and themed days

___Fun competitions

___Volunteer opportunities

What's your score?
I scored TKO Graphix a 70. We're strong in some areas of employee engagement and have room for improvement in others. How did you score your organization, and more importantly, what did it show you? Did you recognize areas for improved employee engagement? Did you see obvious areas in need of improvement? If so, is it time to get started, or do you want to form a committee to discuss it for a few months?

Are you ready to make a difference?
The facts are in: Employee engagement reduces turnover, improves production, and makes your customers happier. Your organization may be good at employee engagement, but I'll bet it could be better. Am I right? If so, don't try to talk employee engagement done; pick one action from the workplace engagement checklist above and implement it today. Are you up for the challenge? Are you ready to quit talking about employee engagement and do something?

Do you know what improvements your employees believe would help your business? As good as management's intentions might be, sometimes leaders can't see the forest for the trees. I've used the following survey face-to-face, one-on-one with team members and as a fill-in survey emailed to staff. In both cases I've received valuable insights, worthy ideas, and information I didn't have.

Once, while completing surveys with a maintenance team, I learned that a key piece of equipment was malfunctioning. The team had brought it to management's attention months prior, but no action had been taken. Part of why I was there was to help management learn why production had slowed. The faulty piece of equipment was a big part of the reason. The company bought a new machine and production improved. However, it wasn't only due to the new equipment, but also because the team believed the company cared. They had been listened to and action had been taken.

Chapter 4

Improvement Survey

Name_____ Date_____

Position _____Tenure_____

Responsibilities

_____
_____
_____
_____

How would you improve your job? The company?

_____
_____
_____
_____

What tools are needed improve the workplace?

_____
_____
_____
_____

What training would improve the workplace?

_____
_____
_____
_____

Training

What would you do differently?

_____
_____
_____
_____
_____

If you were the manager, how would you manage differently?

_____
_____
_____
_____
_____

What would you tell your manager to make them a better manager?

_____
_____
_____
_____
_____

What makes you happy or unhappy at work?

_____
_____
_____
_____
_____

Chapter 4

What's the best part of the job?

_____
_____
_____
_____
_____

What's the worst part of the job?

_____
_____
_____
_____
_____

What should I ask that I didn't ask you?

_____
_____
_____
_____
_____

Cross-Training in Action

A couple of years ago, I facilitated a one-hour training session on silo busting with 12 Stars Media (www.12starsmedia.com). A video production company, 12 Stars Media is known for its teamwork but wanted to take its team from good to great. During the meeting, I offered a dozen silo-busting methods. The team took notes, appointed group leaders, and set up a meeting to choose one action to take. Here's what Zach Downs, 12 Stars Media COO, had to share about their silo-busting team-building process.

Take a Walk in the Other Person's Shoes

by Zach Downs

A sales guy working with a back-end web developer. The accounting manager working with a videographer. Sound bizarre and almost useless? Maybe at first, but let's take a closer look.

But first, let's take a step back and talk about how "job shadowing" started at 12 Stars Media.

Silo Busting!

My co-founder (Rocky) and I wanted to somehow improve teamwork within 12 Stars Media. We tossed around some ideas, but we knew we wanted to bring in an outside party to 1) provide fresh ideas and 2) give input and opinions to the team that weren't from me or Rocky. A good friend of ours, Randy Clark, has been presenting about teamwork and leadership for a while, so we were lucky enough to have him come in and talk to all our team members about silo busting. *Silo busting* means breaking down barriers between the various departments within an organization to improve collaboration and efficiency.

Randy mentioned several activities during his presentation, but the one that really stood out to us was job shadowing. While the idea of job shadowing wasn't new to us, we needed to know where to start. Randy suggested we designate a group of various team members to be in charge of meeting and discussing how we would implement job shadowing into our organization.

Things got off to a great start. We pulled team members from different departments to plan out this new initiative, which was totally outside of their day-to-day activities. This gave us some really great input on what our team had questions about, what they wanted to learn, and how they wanted to learn. To get job shadowing started, every team member drew a name from a hat and shadowed that person before our monthly "huddle" (team meeting), which worked great.

While job shadowing is tracked, and we acknowledge team members when they do it, it is optional. We knew if someone was uninterested in doing an activity, it would ultimately be useless. However, nearly all of our team members have participated in three or more job shadowing activities over the past six months.

Some Solutions

Playing around with cameras, seeing how social engagement tools work, learning what PHP is, and viewing a sales proposal as it's being assembled is fun and all, but where is the value to the company? Well, we have a simple document that we call a "solution brief" that explains it.

We strongly encourage every team member to fill out solution briefs regularly, especially during and immediately after shadowing a team member. This is an awesome way to get a new perspective on things we do every day. For example, our lead developer, who is normally very disconnected from video shoots, came up with the idea to label dead camera batteries while he was shadowing on a video shoot. It's a simple suggestion, but something that our production team hadn't thought of before. Now, it's incredibly easy to know which batteries are charged and which are dead, all because of this one shadowing activity.

The Results

It doesn't take up much time to enable great learning and collaboration opportunities. We've had over 50 job-shadowing activities logged since the rollout in April of 2014, which has resulted in just under a 20-minute average of job-shadowing per team member per month.

Here are some of the direct benefits we've experienced:

Fresh perspective on processes, which results in identification of areas with room for improvement.

Team collaboration, which results in immediate improvement in morale (because it's always a fun break from day-to-day activities to watch what someone else does), but also in the long term because it enables two team members who typically don't collaborate (or even communicate) to be put into an environment where they can build a relationship.

Training for team members, which results in improved skills that, for us, typically means better video production value for our clients.

Job shadowing is self-motivated — no one is required to do it — which is great for Rocky and me because we don't have to manage much of it at all. We do meet once a month with each member of our team individually to discuss their job-shadowing activities (as well as other KPIs). We feel like this is a crucial step to keeping our team motivated and feeling acknowledged for job shadowing.

Just because you have improvement opportunities revealed doesn't mean anything will get better; it's up to those in management to take that information and implement changes. But if you're willing to put forth the effort, it is certainly worth the results.

Is Your Company Improving, and Will It Last?

A wise man once told me that in business, as in life, there's no such thing as stagnant; you're either on the way up or on the way down. In business, how does one gauge improvement? The most obvious answer is net receipts. Is the company growing, and is it profitable? That may be the most conclusive measurement; without profit, all else eventually fails. But is profitable growth sustainable? Are the procedures and people in place to continue the progress? How can a company continue to improve?

It begins with honest assessment. To sustain continuous improvement, an organization must look hard and deep into its culture, systems, and personnel, forming vision teams,[15] conducting SWOT analyses,[16] analyzing results, and implementing initiatives.

Follow through with education. Continuously exposing staff to personal improvement creates a culture of continuous improvement. Leadership training, offsite courses, and brainstorming meetings all contribute to a culture of continuous improvement.

It's about asking questions. Continuous questioning is part of continuous improvement. How can we improve, why do we do it that way, and what are we not doing that we should? These questions are all part of the daily equation.

---

[15] I write more about vision teams at tkographix.com/how-a-vision-team-could-save-your-business.
[16] Learn about SWOT analyses at tkographix.com/how-to-conduct-a-swot-audit.

And then drive activities. Any goal, including continuous improvement, is only a hope and wish without a plan. Base plans on objective criteria — just the facts, ma'am.

- What activities do we need to continue?
- What activities need improvement?
- What activities need to be discontinued?
- What activities need to be reinstated?

Developing a culture of continuous improvement

It's not as easy as it sounds. As much as everyone wants things to improve, most don't want to invest the time needed to do so. For lack of an oil change, the delivery truck engine expired. Why wasn't the oil changed? They were too busy with deliveries. It happens in every organization: Teams become too busy to maintain equipment, train personnel, or question activities. History is littered with profitable companies that didn't maintain their success. There are hundreds of examples of organizations that showed tremendous growth and then faltered. Things change. New technologies replace old, the marketplace ebbs and flows, and what worked a short time ago becomes obsolete. Without a commitment to continuous improvement, it's easy to miss the evolution.

Pick Three ACTION PLAN

Pick three actions to implement over the next 90 days. One to be accomplished in the first 30 days, the second in 60, the third in 90. Each action should be

- Something that's achievable in 30 days or less.

- Activity driven. How will it be accomplished?

- Within your control. Nothing which depends on other departments or corporate approval.

The actions you pick don't have to be earth shattering. Progress and improvement often begin with one small step. You most likely will not have an answer to all the following questions. The idea is to get you thinking about actions that could positively impact you and your team.

What have you put off that you'd like to get done?

_____
_____
_____
_____
_____
_____

What would improve your business?

_____
_____
_____
_____
_____
_____

Chapter 4

> What would help your team?
>
> _____
> _____
> _____
> _____
> _____
>
> What can you and your department do better, more of, more quickly, more cost effectively, or in a more organized way?
>
> _____
> _____
> _____
> _____
> _____
>
> Don't overthink this or make it too difficult. We all have actions we've been meaning to "get to" — what are yours? Good intentions are worthless unless they're acted upon.

Stop Putting Off Your Business Plan

If you're self-employed, even if it's a side hustle, you need a business plan. Whether you're an independent contractor, solopreneur, or chief executive officer of a multimillion-dollar operation — you know you should have a business plan. You may even have one ... you just haven't looked at it in three years. Without a coherent business plan, how can you know where to focus training for yourself and your team?

If you're not using your plan, it may be too complicated for your immediate needs. There's a time and place for a complete business plan. (The U.S. Small Business Administration shows you how to create one quickly at https://www.sba.gov/business-guide/plan-your-business/write-your-business-plan.) If you're presenting to investors, seeking funds from financial institutions, or applying to government agencies, you'll need a complete plan, but it might not be what you need to navigate your day-to-day business.

Why don't you use your plan?
- There's little or no flexibility. If your business plan isn't adaptable to change, opportunities, and threats, it may not help you plan your next step.
- It's not your plan. You hired a consultant or agency to "help" you devise a plan, and at the time it sounded good, but the reality is … it's not your reality.
- Your priorities have changed. A couple of years ago it was what you wanted, but things have changed. Your business has changed, and so have you.

Why don't you have a plan?
- You've convinced yourself you don't need a business plan — you're not big enough and you're doing fine without it.
- You researched creating a business plan, but it was too time consuming and complicated.
- You discussed it with a consultant, but it was too expensive.

What's the answer?
You may not need a full-blown business plan with an executive summary, organizational chart, market analysis, and company description to give your business direction. For your daily business, you may need a simpler, more direct and flexible plan.

- **What do you want to achieve and how will you measure it?** How do you define success? Whether its adding clients, gaining market share, or increasing margins, determine what you want.
- **How will you get there?** Determine what activities you'll need to ramp up, repeat, discontinue, or improve.
- **Adjust it as needed.** Review your business plan at the rate of change in your business. This may sound like overkill, but if your business changes daily, look at your plan daily. For most, a monthly review of the plan will suffice.
- **KISS — keep it simple stupid.** This is your daily business guide, not your official send-this-to-the-bank business plan. It should take minutes, not hours, to review.

Chapter 4

By determining what you want and the activities that will get you there, and consistently reviewing and adjusting the plan, you can develop a business plan that works for you.

When's the last time you looked at your business plan? Taking action without a plan is like throwing darts — if you're lucky, you might hit the bull's-eye, but do you really want the future of your business to be solely determined by luck? What are your goals?

Why SMART Goals Are Dumb

I know I'm bucking the status quo, but as good as SMART goals can be, they have one glaring omission. The SMART goal acronym is credited to Dr. George Doran, who published the concept in 1981. I know you can do the math but think about this: 1981 was 38 years ago. The world is a different place in 2019.

Regardless, what makes SMART goals dumb has always been that you cannot *do* a goal; you have to do activities, and that's where SMART goals come up short.

The SMART goal acronym stands for

S – Specific

M – Measurable

A – Achievable

R – Results Focused

T – Time Bound

There's an expanded version, SMARTER goals:

E – Ethical

R – Recorded

Outlined under the S in SMART goals (specific) are the 5 Ws — *who, what, when, where,* and *which*. *Which* is used to identify outside consequences. But there's a problem: Where is *how*?

One SMART goal tutorial I read gave an example of a poorly written sales goal: to sign up more customers. I agree it's a poorly written goal. However, to make this into a viable goal, the tutorial suggested it be changed to adding two new customers per month. That's not a well-planned goal either; it's a wish. What's missing is *how*.

In this scenario, the *how* might be to cold call five new prospects per day and set two appointments per week. And then follow up on these activities with training and tools to achieve the goal, such as having the manager travel with the salesperson to appointments, conduct cold-call training once per week, and talk with each salesperson about their activities daily.

Activities are hard to find in SMART goals, and that's dumb. Sometimes actions can be found under A — *achievable* — and occasionally they sneak into *specific*, but they're not always there, and the importance of planning activities to reach goals isn't clearly stated in SMART goals.

Don't get me wrong: There's not much I disagree with about SMART goals. Every letter in the acronym is important. It's just that SMART goals miss, or at least downplay, the most critical ingredient of any goal, an action plan — a set of activities to continue, renew, improve, or discontinue. Regardless of how specific, measurable, attainable, results focused, and time bound a goal is, without activities, it's not much more than a hope. And that's dumb.

Effective Goals Are Driven by Activities

7 Goal-Setting Mistakes

Most of us have set goals only to abandon them after the mood has gone. Consider New Year's resolutions. If you're like me, you've failed to follow through on more resolutions than you've succeeded at, but not because you didn't want to achieve the goal. You didn't plan to quit. So, why didn't you hit your goal? The answer might be in one of these seven mistakes.

1. **Don't set too many goals at one time.** For example, resolving to lose weight, learn a language, go back to school, run every day, and cut down on the ole Coors Lite may not be realistic. Pick one and focus on it.

2. **Don't set general, nonspecific goals** — for example, "I'm going to lose weight!" Spell out how much weight, devise your plan of attack, and set a deadline.
3. **Don't wait until it's almost too late.** Don't set unplanned last-minute goals; put a little thought into it before setting a resolution.
4. **Don't bite off more than you can chew.** Break large goals into smaller, achievable bites. For example, if you haven't been running, and you resolve to run a half marathon, you're not going run 13 miles (and 192 yards) next week. If you wanted to write 100 blog posts next year, you wouldn't try to write them all in one month, would you?
5. **Don't keep your goal to yourself.** Go public with your goal. If you're serious about your goal — and by that, I mean you've thought it out and have a plan — then going public may be the added pressure you need to succeed.
6. **I'll say it again.** Do not focus on the goal — focus on activities. You cannot do a goal, but you can do activities.
7. **Don't overcomplicate it.** Keep it simple.

Do the Math

When I was a full-time salesperson, I frequently exceeded my quotas and always came very close to my predicted goals. It wasn't luck. It was achieved by gathering information, following a plan, and putting in the hard work. You can do the same thing. And although I use sales as an example, this system isn't limited to sales. It can be used for anything that can be tracked. For example, I use this system daily to track, pace, and adjust book sales. It can be used for improving the quality of manufactured products, reducing waste, or increasing web contacts. Here's the process.

TRACK IT

What is your *close percentage* — completed orders per sales presentations? Let's start at the beginning — contact. If we define a *contact* as having a conversation with a prospect via email, phone, face to face, or social media, how many contacts does it take to get a lead? If we define a *lead* as a prospect willing to take a presentation, how many leads does it take to gain an order (a sale)? Once you have this basic information, you can formulate the number of contacts needed to hit your quota. For example, if for every 10 contacts you develop one lead and for every five leads you gain one order, it will take 50 contacts to make a sale. If your monthly quota is 10 sales, you'll need to make 500 contacts divided by 25 working days = 20 contacts per day to hit your quota. Do you want to beat your quota? **Do the math.** How many contacts per day would you need to achieve 15 sales in a month?

PACE IT
To avoid confusion, let's stay with a monthly quota of 10 sales. To pace your sales results, take the total number sales made month to date divided by the days worked times the total number of working days for the month. For example, if five days into the month you have two sales that means you have an average of 0.4 (2 ÷ 5) sales per day. Take 0.4 times the total number of workdays, in this case 25, which is 0.4 x 25 = 10 sales. You're on pace to hit your quota of 10 sales. **Do the math.** If your goal is 10 sales in 25 days and you have 4 in the first 12 days, what's your pace?

ADJUST IT
If, at 10 days, you have 3 sales, 3 ÷ 10 = 0.3 x 25 = 7.5 sales, or 2.5 below quota. To hit your quota, you'll need to adjust. If you need 7 sales to hit your quota of 10, and 15 days remain, then you'll need 7 sales in 15 days, or about 1/2 a sale a day. And if it takes 50 contacts to make a sale, you need to increase your contacts from 20 to 25 per day (rounded up). **Do the math**. If you have 10 days remaining in your month-long goal and need 5 more sales, how many sales per day will you need and how many contacts will be required?

Sales has been called a numbers game. There's a lot more to it than numbers, but the numbers are a key element. To set realistic goals, the sales team needs to know the numbers.

Playing by the Numbers
When setting a goal, a good place to start is to look at previous results. For example, if you're setting yearly goals, first review the numbers from the year past.

TOTAL SALES
What was the sales volume the previous year? Can it be repeated or improved upon, and if so, what activities will get you there?

NUMBER OF CALLS TO SET A PRESENTATION
Whether your method is contact by phone, face to face, email, or some other technique, determine how many calls it took to set an appointment. Next, look for actions that might lower the number of contacts needed to create a lead.

Chapter 4

NUMBER OF PRESENTATIONS TO CLOSE A SALE
How many sales presentations did you need to close a sale? Did it require 3 presentations to make a sale? Did you close 2 out of 10? You can use this information to predict how many presentations you'll need to reach your sales goal. For example, if you sold 2 out of 10 presentations, your close rate is 20 percent. If you want to make 20 sales, you'll need to give 100 presentations.

What's your average sale in dollars?

What was the value of the average order last year? Was it $5,000 or $25,000, and can it be improved?

Once you have the numbers, you can do the math and calculate the number of calls you'll need to make to hit your goal.

For example, with a **goal for the year of $500,000 in net sales,** at an **average sale** of $13,500, 37 sales will be needed to reach the goal. At a **close percentage** of 20 percent (two out of ten presentations resulting in a sale), you'll need 185 presentations to reach 37 sales.

If the rate of **presentations set per call** is 10 percent (for every ten calls one presentation is set), you'll need to make 1,850 calls to set 185 presentations. With 260 working days on a five-day work week, you'll need to make 8 calls per day to hit the $500,000 goal.

HAVE YOU CALCULATED YOUR GOAL?
If you want to meet and beat your quotas, you'll need to track, pace, and adjust on a daily basis. At first glance, this may look daunting. But once you have the hang of it, it's easy-peasy and well worth the time and effort. If you who use CRM software, it probably does all of these calculations and more for you. However, there are two keys that many miss, whether they use CRM or go old school. I already mentioned the first: TPA (track, pace, and adjust) *daily*. Yes, do this every day. If you want to hit your numbers, get obsessed with TPA.

Second, no computer program or spreadsheet can make the adjustments for you. That's on you, and the bottom line is it will mean a concentrated effort and a lot of hard work, but if you do the math, you can amaze your co-workers and attain your predictions.

Training

I have a challenge for you: Try it for the next 25 days. Regardless of whether you're in sales, administration, or customer service, recognize the objective criteria and then track, pace, and adjust the numbers.

Presentations

Chapter 5

Chapter 5: Presentations

I was having dinner and drinks with a few friends last week when one member of the group brought up having completed her first class as a professor of journalism. She had recently retired from journalism (do journalist ever really retire?) and was teaching a writing class at a local university. My friend wasn't content with only sharing her knowledge; she wanted her students to act. So, she gave them actionable assignments. She was adding action to her words.

For the last few years, I've added action plans to most training sessions and presentations I've given. Whether presenting about business blogging or working with a management team on leadership development, I add actions to my words. I've made mistakes when designing action plans, but I've learned a few things that I can share.

Adding action to a presentation begins by creating and delivering an engaging presentation. If you don't engage your audience, what will they take away? Here are a few points to consider when developing a presentation.

How to Prepare to Present

You aren't alone: Everyone gets the jitters. I haven't met a presenter who didn't. But the more you present, the easier it becomes. You will mess up. You'll omit, forget, and ramble. It's no big deal unless you make it one. Your audience doesn't know, so don't tell them. Don't apologize for your mistakes. Take deep breaths, look toward the audience, even if it's at a spot on the back wall, and smile. If you're prepared, if you take the time to practice, presenting can be a fun, rewarding, and fulfilling experience.

Nothing beats preparation

A killer presentation doesn't just happen. It takes forethought, inspiration, hard work, planning, and practice. Here are a few steps to planning your next presentation.

Steps to planning a presentation

- **Outline the presentation.** Although you could write out your presentation word for word, I advise against it. It adds an unnecessary level of difficulty, and the presentation often comes off stiff and phony. Make an outline, bullet the key points, and add thoughts.
- **Avoid a boring lecture.** Ask questions throughout your presentation. How can more questions be added? Review every statement and ask if it would improve the presentation if re-formed as a question. Use open-ended questions — who, what, and how — to solicit more than yes and no answers. Walk the room before the presentation, ask questions, and consider whom to call on.
- **Tell stories.** Give examples, share personal experiences, and tell stories others have told you. Stories can add credibility and help define your subject. Should you tell humorous stories? You can, but you don't have to unless it's appropriate and you're good at.
- **Use multimedia.** Grab as many senses as you can. Have something to put in your audience's hand, such as a brochure, a fill-in-the-blank sheet, or an action plan, and use Prezi or PowerPoint.
- **Practice, practice, practice, practice, practice,** and then practice some more. I can't say it enough. The best way to overcome fear of failure is preparation. Don't practice until you get it right, practice until you can't get it wrong.

I've been asked how I psyche myself up immediately before I present. Do I listen to certain music, meditate, or have a cocktail? I've tried all three, but what works best for me is to rehearse my opening on the way to the presentation, to arrive early, and to meet the audience. If you're prepared and comfortable with your audience, you will do well.

3 Steps to Preparing a Killer Presentation

Okay, if you google how to give a presentation, there's like a million and one hits, so why one more? Because I'm not going to tell you it's all about your PowerPoint, the clothes you wear, or how you use a microphone. All those things are important, but together, they won't make for a killer presentation. Preparing a killer presentation is more personal.

Memorize names, faces, and responsibilities
Recently, while presenting about leadership to a small business, I went around the table and recognized each of the dozen or so attendees by name and their position within the organization. Before any meeting I facilitate with an organization, I go to their website and review their About page. Most About pages include a meet-the-team section with photos and titles. Last year, I presented to a leadership organization with more than 40 active members. I greeted most of them by name. People are a lot more responsive to what you have to share when you take the time to learn who they are.

I attended a lecture on small business sponsored by a local financial institute; there were 10 attendees. The speaker introduced herself and then went around the table having everyone introduce themselves. Later she attempted to engage individuals, which is a good thing. However, she would call on people by their clothing, for example, "Orange sweater, what would you do?" It didn't go over well.

Engage your audience
I conducted a leadership development meeting with a group of 11 managers last week. It was the third presentation I'd given to this group. Near the end, one of the attendees told me how much she enjoyed my presentations. "The hour goes by fast and is never boring," she said. I asked her how she thought I accomplished this, and she said, "Because you ask us questions."

Conversely, I attended a discussion where the facilitator spent the first 15 minutes lecturing, and then took over the conversation, occasionally asking leading questions such as, "You agree, don't you?"

Engaging your audience isn't complicated: ask them questions, learn what they know, and help them solve problems.

Have fun
Have you ever begun a meeting with an icebreaker? It's a fun way to get a meeting started. I attended a meeting of nine where the leader divided the attendees into three

teams. Each was given a deck of cards and then told they had five minutes to build the tallest card house possible. It was interesting to watch these leaderless groups in action, how they innovated, communicated, and worked together. It was fun.

I like to poke fun at myself when I'm presenting. At a meeting I was giving, I admitted that I had deleted the word *rural* from my outline because it was difficult for me to pronounce. I went on to awkwardly attempt to say it. The group laughed with me; several agreed that they found it difficult to pronounce as well, and it helped us bond.

Are you ready to create a killer presentation?

Creating a killer presentation is more than writing an outline and producing visuals. Many presenters think that's all it takes, but that's only the beginning. Regardless of how professional you are, if you don't know your audience, engage them, send a call to action, and have fun, then you might have a good presentation but not a memorable one. Do you want to kill your next presentation? If so, you know what to do.

How to Be an Engaging Presenter

I've been privileged to co-present with my good friend Allison Carter. She's a talented and passionate person who I'm lucky enough to call my friend. One of the best things about sharing a presentation, besides working with Allison, was that I learned something about presenting, which surprised me, although it shouldn't have. I learned how audience engagement could be used to deliver a message.

A few years ago, we presented together on the topic of taking your online networking offline from the points of view of a young introvert and an old extrovert.[17] In preparation, we talked about the subject, sent emails with ideas back and forth, outlined the presentation, and role-played. Then we role-played some more. We put enough thought and effort into the presentation to make it look effortless.

What's the key?

One of the keys to our presentation was engaging the audience in networking. Near the end of the presentation, we had people change seats and introduce themselves, and we gave them a couple of questions to ask each other. We had similar results at five different

---

[17] Read "Taking Social Networking Face-to-Face" at blog.tkographix.com/taking-social-networking-face-to-face.

venues where we presented. The attendees got so into it that we were forced to interrupt their conversation to continue our presentation. Not only that, but people would stay after our presentation to continue their chats.

What was our plan?
- We arrived early and networked with attendees as they arrived. We asked what expectations they had, what would help them, how they used social networks, what networking challenges they faced, and what successes they might share.
- We geared the presentation as much as possible to the specific audience based on what we learned before the presentation.
- We called on members of the audience who had shared with us.
- We asked open-ended *what*, *why*, and *how* questions throughout the presentation. Sometimes simply changing a question from "Are there any questions?" to "What questions do you have?" made a difference.
- We shook things up. In our case by passing out numbered action sheets and then asking all who had an odd-numbered sheet to switch tables and seats.
- We gave assignments. Ours was simply having the participants ask each other, "How can I help you?" After giving the assignments, Allison and I would stand at the front of the group, smiling at the engagement we observed.

Eventually we learned we needed to set time limits or we'd run out of time. So, what did we learn about presenting? If you want to be an engaging presenter, engage your audience. Don't talk at them — talk with them.

Adding Stories and Questions to Your Presentation

If you want to be a more engaging presenter, add stories and questions to your presentation.

I'm in the process of facilitating a series of management development sessions with the TKO Graphix installation team leaders. We have installation managers all around Indiana — in Plainfield, the south side of Indianapolis, Lafayette, Terre Haute, and Brazil. The group numbers more than a dozen, so we split them into two teams for training purposes, meeting every other week with each group.

Chapter 5

Management training was something new for most of the team managers. They haven't been through a lot of management training, so we decided to walk them through my *New Manager's Workbook*. Although I wrote the book and have used it countless times in group meetings, I practiced the presentation twice before giving it once again.

When the meeting was over, installation manager Bill Moss and I discussed the presentation. I asked what I could improve. He didn't have anything for me, to which I answered, "That doesn't help me." And then he shared that his goal was to be able to give the level of seminar that I had just completed. He told me that he knew the material, and often had stories and examples, but he'd forget them or get off track.

I asked Bill how he prepared to talk. He told me that at first, he tried writing it out word for word, but that put too much pressure on him, and it sounded like he was a bad actor reading a script. Bill asked me how I kept track of my stories, questions, and anecdotes. Here's what I told him:

1. **Outline your meeting.** I agreed that writing a script never worked for me. It sounded phony, as if it was … scripted. I told Bill that I outline the key points I want to touch on.
2. **Add stories.** I showed Bill my handwritten outline and where on the outline I added stories to my notes. I simply draw a square and then add a title to the story as a reminder. For example, if I were presenting on how I outline a meeting, I might add a square with the title "Bill on adding stories." My first review of any presentation outline is to look for opportunities to add appropriate stories.
3. **Change statements to questions.** The next thing I showed Bill were questions I added to the outline. I reviewed the entire outline looking for places I could change a statement to a question — usually an open-ended one.
4. **Practice.** I told Bill that although I had covered this material more times than I could count, I still practiced it before presenting. For example, I had given this presentation to the other half of the group the previous week, but because this was a different group, and I wanted to fit the needs of this team, I rehearsed the talk out loud twice before I gave it.

When Bill and I finished talking, he thanked me. I could see from his expression that he understood that what I did wasn't magic. It was preparation. Bill knew he could do the same. As he left, he told me he was inspired. The truth is it was Bill who inspired me. It's why I do this.

Adding Action to My Fort Wayne TEDx

A few years ago, I was privileged to speak at TEDx Fort Wayne. My talk was about building community by engaging friends in help and action. It was about the brainstorming group I belong to — Friend Up.

I shared how Friend Up began and how to create a Friend Up group. It's simple: You pick a time and place, invite friends, ask them for one or two areas where they could use help, choose a facilitator, brainstorm, take notes, and then post calls to action and advice on a private group.

The facilitator leads the discussion by:

- Asking, "How can we help?"
- Following up with open-ended questions — what, how, and why.
- Seeking the group's thoughts, ideas, and advice.

I had asked friends from my Friend Up group to define Friend Up, and during my TEDx talk, I shared their definitions. Here's what some of them said:

> The people that I have met in the Friend Up group have helped to promote my various volunteer/work projects. Not only have these incredible individuals tweeted and liked, but they have rolled up their sleeves and pitched in as well. It is through their direct efforts that these initiatives have been successful. —Bethann Buddenbaum

> "The best Friend Ups have a core group of people who listen to each other and are willing to offer help, suggestions, and ideas to one another. Meeting on a monthly basis is supplemented by conversations via social media and even in person or phone. One of the true keys is giving — a spirit of helping each other — as opposed to taking — what's in it for me?" —Scott Howard

> "A Friend Up means more than social media, business development, or networking. I think the fact that it has *friend* in the name is important despite that it's easy to overlook or take for granted as a generic term. The people at a Friend Up are friends first, then everything that comes from that

is more meaningful and valuable than what I've experienced at many other similar types of events that don't place quality, friendly relationships at the forefront of their purposes." —Rocky Walls

Then I added action to my words. Near the end of my time, I asked the audience if they'd considered Fort Wayne TEDx a networking opportunity. Most did. Then I asked them to stand up, turn to someone, introduce themselves, and ask, "How can I help you?" Next, I asked them to inquire, "What person, company, or industry would you like to be introduced to?"

In the end, I had to interrupt them so I could finish my talk on time. I don't know what connections were made and actions taken, but it was a good start.

If you'd like to see it, you can watch the last two minutes of my talk at TEDX Fort Wayne online at www.youtube.com/watch?v=y-6o1GjAGoA.

Leadership Hendricks County

For the last couple of years, I've had the pleasure of presenting to Leadership Hendricks County. I enjoy working with this group. It's filled with people wanting to be better people — leaders who want to improve their leadership skills and who commit to taking action.

Both years I've presented on conflict resolution. I introduced myself and then shared my goal that every member of the leadership group pick one thing to commit to acting on. I shared ideas about conflict resolution, such as the Pinch Method of Conflict Resolution. We discussed when corrective action was called for and appropriate. I shared how to do a sandwich method critique. We discussed what to do when working with someone is killing you, and I asked if it's possible to make everybody happy and then shared actions that could be used to mitigate problems.

At the end, I asked each of the 25 or so in attendance for their takeaway. They were enthusiastic and ready to act on their commitments. Here's my point: I have given hundreds of presentations where I did not seek to engage the audience to solidify my message, talks where I didn't offer takeaways, and sessions when I didn't ask for commitments to action. I have to wonder if those talks made a difference or influenced any of the attendees.

Indianapolis Department of Metropolitan Development

Last summer, I presented to a group of approximately 30 members of the Indianapolis Department of Metropolitan Development. Their mission is to guide the future of metropolitan Indianapolis by "creating affordable homeownership opportunities and supporting the growth of jobs and investment in our community. The Department of Metropolitan Development works in partnership with other city departments to build a world-class city, neighborhood by neighborhood."

I introduced myself with a short résumé of my leadership experience. Next, I mentioned my two leadership books and that they were based on my many management mistakes. I discussed my expectations of the attendee's participation and questions (there is no dumb question). And then I shared my goal. I explained that if all we did today was for me to stand at the podium and lecture, then not much would be accomplished. Therefore, my goal was for each person to choose one actionable item from the presentation. I explained that, at the end of my talk, I'd go around the room and ask each person for their takeaway.

I proceeded with my presentation, sharing the idea that projects can be managed, but people should be led or influenced. I shared what makes someone worth following: It's not a title, or money, or charisma. Next, we discussed assumptions made by inexperienced managers and followed up with 10 ways to be a better boss. I ended my part of the presentation by highlighting activities great leaders avoid. Throughout the presentation, I handed out fill-in-the-blank one-pagers that followed my presentation. As I talked, I reminded everyone of my goal and explained that they might find an actionable item on any of the one-pagers or they could be inspired to create a plan.

With about 15 minutes to go, I went around the room and asked each attendee for their plan. Everyone participated, some enthusiastically. I believed some of the action plans might benefit from one of my books, so I gave a few away. I don't know who followed up with their commitments and who did not. However, I heard enough passion, saw enough commitment, watched as many took notes, and responded to enough thoughtful questions to know some action was taken, and that's certainly better than me standing at the podium and talking for an hour, isn't it?

Chapter 5

Whether you're training, presenting, or conducting a meeting, if what you're doing is standing at the podium and talking for an hour, then you should ask yourself how much the audience is getting out of your speech. And then add action to your next talk.

Young Business Leaders Presentation

A few years ago, I was asked by an organization to replace a presenter who had canceled the week of his presentation. I had four days to prepare. I agreed.

I was to speak to a group of young professionals. After learning the general makeup of the group, I decided to forgo any of the several presentations I had previously prepared.

I was nearing the completion of a management workbook. At the time, it contained 11 modules comprising 35,000 words on how to be an effective manager. As a management consultant, I had seen too many organizations that trained managers by osmosis. A newly promoted manager would be told to hire, train, complete a corrective action, or conduct a meeting with little more direction than, "Here's the form; fill it out and make me a copy." I decided to base my presentation on the workbook in progress.

I arrived before the luncheon. I didn't eat, but as people arrived, I introduced myself and asked about their profession and position and if they managed direct reports. Then I asked each their greatest management challenge. I heard conflict management, delegation, working as a team, but almost everyone mentioned communication. At that time, there wasn't much in my workbook about communication, and I was standing in front of a room full of young professionals who wanted to improve their team's communication. What was I to do? I suggested ideas, asked others for input, and then I shared what had worked for me in business communication.

And, I added a chapter on communication to the workbook. I want to thank Muncie Young Professionals for inviting me to speak and for inspiring me.

Presentations

The bottom line is that building presentations as if they were mini-workshops works. Ask people to participate before and during the presentation, hand out action plan sheets, share slides, and ask questions throughout the presentation. And then finish by asking attendees to commit to an action.

Presentations

Presentation Outline Form

Opening: Include objective and goal (for each to commit to an action)

_____
_____
_____
_____

Outline Points: Share 3 to 5 points to be covered in the presentation.

1. _____
2. _____
3. _____
4. _____
5. _____

Go into detail on each point

_____
_____
_____
_____
_____
_____
_____
_____
_____

Review and summarize each point

_____
_____
_____
_____

Chapter 5

_____
_____
_____
_____
_____

Close by restating your objective and goal

_____
_____
_____
_____

Call to action: Ask for commitments to act

_____
_____
_____
_____

Seminars and Workshops

Chapter 6

Chapter 6: Seminars and Workshops

A Half-Day Workshop

I was asked by a top-100 *Engineering News-Record* construction company for my advice on content marketing. Before the workshop, I talked with two key members of the team, and then followed up with a questionnaire. Below is the completed questionnaire (answers are in italics).

I include this survey not so you have a questionnaire for content marketing; it's to show how a detailed survey can inform and direct any workshop. The completed survey helped me create a workshop geared to the company's specific needs, not a one-size-fits-all presentation. As you review the survey, stop and consider how you could use surveys to focus presentations on the audience's needs.

Content marketing strategy survey

Content marketing is the sharing of published website content via social media with the purpose of driving traffic directly to the website, improving search engine optimization, and unifying the brand. Content strategy can also be used for customer service initiatives and employee engagement.

- What is the primary purpose of your website?
  To validate to clients our depth of experience and capabilities.
- Who do you want to reach through social media?
  Clients, partner design firms, subcontractors

Chapter 6

- What actions do you want readers to take from your blog?
  Showcase expertise in specific markets (life sciences, healthcare, higher education, parking, cultural, industrial/manufacturing, power)
- What are your biggest content marketing challenges?
  Getting blog information, timing on keeping up with social media, agreement on what should be there
- What tools do you use (for example, TweetDeck, Hootsuite, WordPress)?
  WordPress
- How much time do you spend weekly on content marketing?
  2 hours
- How often do you post, share, and publish on the website, blog, or social media?
  Working on a plan now
- What interferes with your content marketing initiatives?
  Deadlines and other initiatives
- Where do you need help, training, or tools?
  Strategy for when, where, what, and how often
- What would you like to add?

The questionnaire was completed by the head of the marketing department. I asked if she felt comfortable sharing her answers with the team. She did, and she forwarded the document to her teammates, asking for their opinions and advice.

I began the workshop discussing the questionnaire, which led to a conversation about their content marketing priorities as a team. Number one on the list was consistently publishing on the company blog. What was needed was a plan or system that covered the when, where, how, and what of creating and consistently publishing content.

I used my book *How to Stay Ahead of Your Business Blog Forever* to guide them in creating a new blogging plan. We began by choosing four topics, what WordPress calls categories. Then we discussed blog ideas, including FAQs, behind the scenes stories, customer spotlights, and how-to posts. Next, we decided to publish one new blog post per week and created an editorial calendar. The group chose to use Microsoft Outlook because of their familiarity and the ease of sharing the calendar. I recommended they have four to eight posts completed and ready to publish before they post the first one.

Getting ahead of the game relieves pressure and is a primary ingredient to staying ahead of a blog. We also talked about their target audience, editing, social media, and content beyond the blog.

At the end of the day, they had a plan with commitments from the entire team. They had chosen four topics, eight blog post ideas with specific writers for each, and a schedule. We did more than talk. We developed a plan of action.

Communicating with Customers

As part of a continuing workshop on customer service with a retail operation, I facilitated a seminar on how to communicate positively with customers. We covered how to use voice, body language, facial expressions, and word usage.

The ideas were presented in the workshop, and examples were given and then role-played. Prior to the workshop, I asked a few senior members of the staff to help me by sharing good and bad examples. Next, we went around the room on each point and practiced.

I almost always get some resistance when I initiate role playing. I hear, "I can't do it in front of people, but I do it on the job," or "I'm too shy," or some version of "What's this got to do with the job? This isn't real." I've learned it's best to ward this off these types of complaints by explaining the following:

- It's only us and we're all here to learn, not judge.
- You'll probably make mistakes, but that's okay; it's a way to learn.
- If you can do it here, you can do it anywhere.

Explaining the purpose of the role playing doesn't always eliminate objections, but it helps.

After the classroom, we took the lessons to the floor with customers. Managers offered positive reinforcement, encouragement, and constructive criticism. They were doing more than talking about customer service.

Here's the handout I used in the workshop.

Chapter 6

Example Handout: Customer Contact Best Practices

Smile. It's hard not to be positive with a smile on your face. Try it. And isn't that how you want to greet customers — with enthusiasm?

Make eye contact. People don't always trust folks who don't make eye contact. Not a good message to share.

Use lowered inflection. Lowered inflection, when our voices begin on a higher note and descend, is what we use when we're confident. The opposite, rising inflection, is when your voice begins low and the notes rise as you speak. Rising inflection denotes a lack of confidence or a questioning.

Be precise. Don't ramble. Get to the point. Don't chase customers away by being a bore.

Speak clearly. Don't mumble, and don't talk while chewing gum, eating a sandwich, or drinking a soda.

Avoid slang. Speak professionally — be a businessperson.

Never be inappropriate. This includes humor. I was in a retail store with a friend one time when a young man working there said, "Hi, Beautiful!" to my friend. She walked over and said rather curtly, "My name is Becky," and walked away. She hasn't been back to the store since.

Don't be rude. Don't be short or dismissive with customers.

Don't be snarky. A retail market isn't the place to use snark and sarcasm, even if you're trying to be funny.

Don't let negative emotions show in your voice. If you're upset or angry, don't let it show in your voice. Keep a smile on your face and your voice at an even tone.

Set the tone. By sharing a friendly smile, speaking clearly in confident tones, and making eye contact, you can win the ear and the trust of the customer, and isn't that the goal?

More than talk

Had the workshop ended with a handout, lecture, and Q & A, how much progress toward improved customer service would've been made? I don't have the answer, but I know this: By adding role playing and real customer interaction to the workshop, customer service was improved.

How to plan a workshop that makes a difference

Planning a workshop that makes an impact begins with understanding the challenges and needs of the group attending the workshop. This can be accomplished through

- **Observation.** Frequently, I'll pay an unannounced visit to an organization I'm about to consult to get a feel for what they do and how they do it.
- **A survey.** Survey the team by asking for their advice as well as their needs. (See the example survey below.)
- **A meeting with leadership.** Schedule a meeting with senior staff to discuss challenges and expectations.

Example Employee Survey

Our company has certain beliefs and values at the core of our business. These values aren't only what we believe, but they're what has made our organization successful and helped us grow. However, management isn't in the trenches. We don't always know the daily interactions of our company, but you do. We'd like your opinion on five cultural values. We're not asking you to grade yourself but the company overall.

On a scale of 1–10, with 10 being the most positive, how would you rate the company's compliance to the following values?

1. We live by the belief that the customer comes first.

[1] [2] [3] [4] [5] [6] [7] [8] [9] [10]

Comment

_____
_____
_____
_____
_____

2. The accuracy on our orders is about as good as it can be.

[1] [2] [3] [4] [5] [6] [7] [8] [9] [10]

Comment

_____
_____

Chapter 6

_____
_____
_____
_____

3. Communication between departments and with clients is timely and complete.

[1] [2] [3] [4] [5] [6] [7] [8] [9] [10]

Comments

_____
_____
_____
_____
_____

4. Most employees are friendly and helpful to customers, venders, and each other.

[1] [2] [3] [4] [5] [6] [7] [8] [9] [10]

Comments

_____
_____
_____
_____
_____

5. Delivering the best possible product to consumers is always our goal.

[1] [2] [3] [4] [5] [6] [7] [8] [9] [10]

Comments

_____
_____
_____
_____
_____

A Workshop Plan Example

This example is for a sensitivity workshop plan that was completed with a retail organization.

The plan: Cultural sensitivity and inclusion training

The purpose of cultural sensitivity training is to increase the cultural awareness of the staff, train sensitivity best practices, limit exposure while helping to prevent civil rights violations, promote teamwork, and grow the base of loyal customers across multiple cultures.

This will be accomplished by training staff members to recognize cultural differences and implement best practices for working with multiple ethnicities, races, and cultures.

Management staff meeting

The initial meeting was conducted with management and leadership staff. It included parts A and B (see below) with discussion on how to implement the training with staff members.

Employee training

A. **Understanding cultural sensitivity in the workplace.** In this presentation, employees were introduced to federal regulations in the workplace and the organization's belief in and support of cultural sensitivity. The purpose of the presentation was to make employees aware of cultural sensitivity and to limit the organization's exposure to civil rights violations.

B. **Sensitivity training.** This covered how to interact with multiple cultures and create an inclusive environment, how to communicate both verbally and non-verbally in a diverse workplace, and how to avoid categorizing people and to look to each as an individual.

The intent of the workshop was to focus on sensitivity training as opposed to diversity training. Recent studies, including a report from the Harvard Business Review, "Diversity Training Doesn't Work."[18] have shown that diversity training may backfire by pointing out our differences through categorization. Sensitivity training is based on

---

[18] hbr.org/2012/03/diversity-training-doesnt-work

the idea that we are all more than our cultures and background. We're all individuals and should be treated as such. And that's a worthwhile topic to share.

Workshop Outline

Introduction: Introduce the workshop, including objective, goals (takeaways), and agenda

_____
_____
_____
_____

Outline the facilitator's role

- Keep the workshop on topic
- Manage time
- Engage all attendees
- Answer questions

Discuss the importance of attendees' participation and interaction

_____
_____
_____
_____

Review housekeeping and preparation

- **Be on time.** It's unfair to make others wait on late participants or repeat what's been covered before they arrived.
- **Turn off devices.**
- **Call for questions.** Share your expectations of questions.
- **Set up a "parking lot"** where questions that will be answered later in the workshop can be listed.
- **Share materials such as handouts.**

CTA: Ask for commitments to take action from each attendee.

Seminar Outline

Introduce the topic

Share the goal of the seminar (a commitment to act)

Outline 3 to 5 points

Review each point in detail

Chapter 6

Conclude with a summary of each point

_____
_____
_____
_____
_____
_____
_____

Gain commitments to act

Facilitate Q & A

Content

Chapter 7

Chapter 7: Content

Calls to action can be part of most copy. It can be as simple as a CTA choice at the end of a blog post or as complicated as a guide — for example, *Asking the Right Questions: A Guide to Critical Thinking* by M. Neil Browne and Stuart Keeley,[19] which is full of practice exercises that become examples of the critical thinking actions shared throughout the book.

Below is an example of a blog post about reducing stress at work, but it could be almost any topic. I include it here not to discuss stress but as an example of including calls to action in a blog post. How many CTAs can you identify in this post?

Example Post

Stop Stressing Out at Work Now![20]

To stop stressing out and manage stress at work, you first must recognize triggers and reinforcements. Typical ways people excuse stress include, "It's part of the job," "It's just the way I am," "It's only temporary," and "It's caused by others." Regardless how accurate these may sound, all excuses reinforce stress — anything used to justify reduced performance is an excuse and is therefore a source of stress.

How to take away your stress excuses

---

[19] www.pearson.com/us/higher-education/program/PGM329006.html
[20] tkographix.com/stop-stressing-out-at-work-now

Chapter 7

One of the best ways to take away excuses is to analyze your stress by keeping a stress journal. Here's how:

- Track the cause of stress.
- Note how you feel, your emotional state of mind.
- Recognize how you responded.
- Consider what makes you feel better.

How to relieve stress

One of the most effective tools for reducing stress is the Avoid, Alter, Adapt, and Accept system. The system can be used to help you understand your sources of stress and how to channel that stress toward more productive emotions.

Avoid

- **Say no.** Learn to say no when you are at your limit or when it's not your field of expertise.
- **Avoid destructive behavior.** Avoid things such as drugs, alcohol, tobacco, overeating, too much TV, anger.
- **Avoid people who create stress.** We all know them. A couple of weeks ago, a good friend and I went for a hike. We talked about her awakening in 2012 to the people in her life who were causing her stress and how cutting them out (so-called friends) and cutting some back (family) improved her life.
- **Control your environment.** For example, if you hate the evening car crash and house fire fest more popularly known as local TV news, turn it off.
- **Avoid hot buttons.** Controversial topics are so called for a reason. Politics and religion get most people going, so don't start.
- **Distinguish** *must* **do from** *should* **do.**

Alter

- **Let feelings out.** Try the Pinch Method of Conflict Resolution. (Learn more from my post "Are You Using the Pinch Theory of Conflict Management?" at tkographix.com/are-you-using-the-pinch-theory-of-conflict-management.)

- **Compromise.** Don't be like Congress; compromise for the good of all and to relieve stress.
- **Use good time management.**

Adapt

- **Reframe.** For example, change road rage to mindful driving. (If you're interested, read my post "How to be a Mindful Driver" at tkographix.com/mindful-driver.)
- **Look for the big picture.** At the end of the day, how critical was it?
- **Adjust standards.** You don't always have to be perfect.
- **Focus on positives and be appreciative.**

Accept

- **Remember that you can't control the uncontrollable.**
- **Forgive.** Forgiveness isn't about others; it's about you and the stress it relieves.
- **View stressful situations as learning opportunities.**
- **Share with a trusted friend face to face.**
- **Write it out and then throw it away.**

Other stress relievers

There's more to relieving stress at work than the aforementioned. Stress at home and lifestyle choices affect work. If you want to improve stress at work, you should improve how you handle stress in your life.

- Spend time in nature
- Exercise
- Spend time with friends
- Create — arts, crafts, stories
- Enjoy a pet

- Plant a garden

- Find the humor — make fun of yourself

- Read a book

- Listen to music

- Schedule time to relax

- Do something you like every day

- Eat healthy

- Reduce caffeine

- Be around positive people

- Stop worrying. (Any worry can be put in one of two categories: You can either do something about it — so do it — or you can do nothing about — so quit wasting your time and causing stress.)

- Tell your inner voice no. (Our inner voice is there to protect us. It will take limited information and project possible destructive outcomes. As helpful as it may be at times, our inner voice can be a source of stress. Occasionally you must tell the voice, "Thank you but, no, I got this!")

A call to action

Are you ready to tackle stress? Tired of being stressed out? It really is up to you. It's time to take your first small steps toward stress relief. Here's a place to start:

- Identify your top two sources of workplace stress.

- Understand what's reinforcing the behavior. What excuses do you make for stress?

- Plan an action to relieve stress. There are 34 listed above.

- Choose a lifestyle stress reliever. What can you do at home to relieve stress?

- Pick a stress buddy. It should be someone you trust, whom you can talk to face-to-face, and who won't allow you to turn it into a gossipy bitch session.

Can a Book Take Action?

So, can a book take action? Of course not, but it can promote action and encourage action. I recently read *Make Peace with Your Mind* by Mark Coleman.[21] Mark is an internationally renowned mindfulness trainer. The book is about learning to control your inner voice, the inner judge. He inspired me to act.

The book works in part because Mark's writing style is sincere and easy to read. But for me, the biggest reason it works is that Mark ends every chapter with what he calls *practice*. Practice is 10 minutes of actions you can take based on what was discussed in the chapter. We've all read books with good intentions of acting, only to find the book on a shelf with no action taken a year later. Mark puts you to work from cover to cover. It works. It's the perfect example of adding action to words in a book.

Taking Action on Business Blogging

As I've mentioned, I wrote a book on business blogging called *How to Stay Ahead of Your Business Blog Forever*. The book is based on a journey I began in June of 2010, when I struggled to publish one new blog post per week, got behind, almost gave up, and then developed a plan to get and stay ahead. Today I publish six new posts per week, and I'm currently three months ahead. I have more than 70 posts ready to publish. I'm not bragging, because anyone with a business blog can do the same. It takes planning and commitment. Much of my journey in blogging has been trial and error, and although my plan works for me, I'm certain it will not fit the needs of every business blogger. Therefore, my book, which is only 98 pages long, includes 23 action plans.

You cannot read my business blogging book and miraculously get ahead of your blog. You must take action. The action plans are devised so each individual can create a business blogging plan that works for them. For example, there are action plans to choose topics, come up with ideas, and create an editorial calendar.

I think the book is a nice read, but without a plan of action, it's not much more than words on a page.

---

[21] www.amazon.com/dp/B01MCTIQ51

Life

Chapter 8

Chapter 8: Life

Are You Waiting for Others to Change?

Gandhi said, "Be the change you wish to see in the world." For a long time, I thought I understood what he meant, but I was only partially enlightened. It wasn't until I faced obstacles that stopped me in my tracks that I began to understand what he meant. Are you waiting for others to change to fit your needs?

How's that plan working for you?
Last week a co-worker complained that another department wasn't giving him all the information he needed. It had been going on for weeks. I asked him what he'd tried to remedy the problem, and he said, "I told them twice, and my rule is, after that, it's on them. I'm not going to do it for them." This strategy has meant he hasn't had the information he needs for several weeks. The person he's hurting the most is himself. He's waiting for others to change to fit his needs.

The Sunday newspaper
Last Sunday I was having breakfast with my father. We rotate restaurants. This week he chose Denny's. I asked if he'd read an article on the sports page of the Sunday paper. He hadn't because the paper was thrown on his porch, not put in the newspaper holder below his mailbox. At 89 years old, my dad is afraid to bend over on his porch for fear of falling.

I suggested we get him one of those grabber sticks, and his first reaction was that it wasn't a bad idea. But then he said no, "They're not doing their job. They need to put it in the box! And if they don't, I'll cancel the paper!" I didn't argue with him, but my dad looks forward to the Sunday morning paper. He plays the word games, reads the sports section, and looks at the grocery ads (he's a retired grocery store owner). If he follows through with his threat, he'll miss all of this. It won't be the newspaper organization that loses, it will be my father.

I'm not throwing any stones
There have been times I've looked at circumstances out of my control and thought, *That's not my responsibility*. And there have been times, more than once, that I've given up trying and begun blaming others for my failure to hit my goals.

When we point fingers and pass the blame — little will change. Only by taking responsibility can change be effected. Don't concentrate on what you cannot control; concentrate on what you can control. If you wait for others to change to meet your expectations ... you may be waiting a long time. It's easy to say it's not your responsibility, or it's someone else's fault, but if that's your plan, you have no plan. How's the idea of expecting others to change to fit your needs working so far?

Make a new plan and put it into action
Whenever we allow circumstances to prevent us from achieving our best, we give ourselves an excuse. And here's the difficult thing: Our excuse may be real, or it might be out of our control, but does that mean we accept it as a reason to give up? Or do we look for a way to improve the situation?

Where Does Help Begin?

Everywhere you look, we all could use help, support, and advice. Take the workplace for instance. What would make your job easier, make you more efficient, or produce a higher-quality product? Where could you use help? Think about that for a minute. We'll come back to this question, but first, what can you do to make *someone else's* job easier, more efficient, or higher quality?

I'm surprised how many people, when asked where they need help, don't know or don't share what they need. Be prepared by knowing what you need. Have the answer to what would make your job and life easier, more efficient, or more productive. If you don't know, whom should you ask? Know the answer. How can you take action if you don't know what action to take?

It starts with you
Where does help begin? You need to be able to communicate your needs; if you don't share your needs, what good is knowing? How can anyone offer you help if you don't share your needs?

One way to get help is to give it. Begin by helping others. It will not always be reciprocated, but it will often be enough to make it worthwhile. Besides, it's a pretty darn fulfilling way to look at life. Who can you help today? What action can you take to help another?

Leadership Doesn't End at the Office

A member of a leadership team I work with told me his 19-year-old college-student daughter had, to his surprise, called to thank him. It seems she had noticed a new dynamic between Dad and her mother. They were getting along better than ever — not that they had severe problems, but according to Dad, he wasn't always a good listener or open to his wife's and daughter's ideas or input. His daughter said she'd seen a change in Dad. He was becoming a better listener and was open to hearing their ideas. In the past, once Dad's mind was set, he closed the doors. He wasn't open for business. Now he was.

Dad's story
As I listened to his story, I thought, *That's wonderful, but what's the connection?* And then he connected the dots for me. He looked me in the eye, shook my hand, and thanked me. He had applied what he was learning in the leadership classes to his relationship with his family, and it had improved his home life. I was grateful he shared the story. It not only made my day; it gave me satisfaction and fulfillment. It's a big reason I conduct leadership training: to watch others grow.

It wasn't the first time I'd heard this from folks in leadership development. Entire classes have talked about how they applied the leadership training to their personal lives. Management development trainees have shared how they improved communication, team building, and silo busting at home, church, and club. I've been told behavior modification, conflict management, and activity-driven goal setting have improved the lives of not only themselves, but their loved ones.

Others have used problem-solving techniques and time-management methods to make things better in all aspects of their life — not just work.

The best you
Striving to be a better leader at work begins with becoming a better human being. Improving who you are doesn't involve punching a time clock. Becoming an upgraded version of yourself, You 2.0, is a 24/7 job. So, if you strive to be a better manager and leader of people, the kickback is that you become a better person in every aspect of your life. Don't you love it?

When You Stop Learning, You Start Dying … and Your Business Does Too

When you and your leadership team stop learning, it's the death knell of your business. Sticking with how you've always done it will lead to a time where those methods are no longer viable. Just ask Blockbuster, Polaroid, or Borders. The only thing that is constant in life, and in business, is change, and if you don't keep up with the changes in your industry, you'll soon be passed by and eventually forgotten. So, where does learning begin? It starts with you.

You can't know it all, so don't be a know-it-all
It's impossible for any one person to know everything. Do you believe you know everything about your business? You just might, but it also might be that your accountant, attorney, insurance carrier, marketing manager, installation crew, and facility maintenance crew know things you don't. So, stop talking and start listening. Quit telling and begin asking. You never know what you might learn.

The five-hour rule
Have you heard of this? It's something Warren Buffett, Bill Gates, and Oprah Winfrey ascribe to. It's a simple plan: commit to five hours of learning per week, one hour per work day. The five-hour rule isn't new; it was Ben Franklin's plan: "Throughout Ben Franklin's adult life, he consistently invested roughly an hour a day in deliberate learning. I call this Franklin's five-hour rule: one hour a day on every weekday. Franklin's five-hour

rule reflects the very simple idea that, over time, the smartest and most successful people are the ones who are constant and deliberate learners." (From Michael Simmons's, "Why Constant Learners All Embrace the 5-hour Rule."[22])

My co-worker Nancy began listening to podcasts on her daily commute, and another friend is reading business books five or more hours per week. You can take online courses, attend seminars, or go to class, but you must commit and follow through with the five-hour rule. Don't talk about it — do it.

Teach, coach, mentor
If you want to learn a subject inside out, teach it. Anyone who has responsibly taught understands this truism. Preparing to be a good instructor teaches trainers more than their students learn. A good mentor not only shares what they've learned, including their mistakes, but also learns from their mentee. Mentees share new perspectives and ask questions that mentors might never have considered.

Fail
Wait What? Yes, fail. If you never fail, you're not trying hard enough. The key to failing is to learn from it. Failure might be the greatest teacher there is, and the fear of failure is a close second.

In his book *Failure: The Secret to Success*[23] (which I highly recommend), author Robby Slaughter shares the idea that to improve, indeed to succeed, we must fail and that the only mistake made from failure is to not use it as a learning opportunity.

Leading your business in learning
If you're not leading your business in learning, then who is? Hopefully, someone on your team, because if not, you might be in more trouble than you know. I'm reminded of a co-worker telling me about a friend who owned an offset print shop. Although he delivered a good product, the business failed after more than 25 years. He told my co-worker that he didn't know what else to do because online stores were putting him out of business, and he didn't have a website.

---

[22] www.inc.com/empact/why-constant-learners-all-embrace-the-5-hour-rule.html
[23] www.failurethebook.com/book/

Looking at it now, it's easy to identify what he should have done, isn't it? But consider this: If you don't commit to continuous learning, you might end up exactly like the print shop owner and not see the end coming until it's too late.

If You Want to Change, Change Your Lifestyle

Where does change begin? It isn't the same for everyone. For some it's a mindset that leads to action. While for others it's more complicated. What works for others won't always work for you. However, change always begins with a plan of action.

My wife has lost more than 20 pounds over the last year. It's not unusual for old friends and acquaintances who haven't seen her for a while to ask her if she's okay. She is. She wasn't obese to begin with, and she wasn't obsessed with losing weight. She just wanted to live a healthier lifestyle.

Competition or lifestyle?
I was the opposite. I joined a weight-loss competition and weighed myself every day, sometimes more than once. I starved myself before weigh-ins, didn't drink water or coffee before I stood on the scales, and took my shoes off. For me, it was more about the competition than an improved lifestyle.

My wife asked me what my weight-loss intentions were, and I told her I wanted to lose weight every week during the contest. Then she asked, "What about after that?" Good question. I hadn't thought that far ahead. I guess I wanted to keep the weight off, but the truth is I'd participated in this group weight-loss effort previously and lost weight, but eventually I put it all back on.

A lifestyle change
My wife looked at me and said, "If you want to live healthier, you won't accomplish it through an eight-week contest. You'll have to change your lifestyle." She was right. I'm working on lifestyle changes. I've cut out several foods that triggered compulsive eating, such as potato chips and cookies. I've reduced late-night snacks, and I'm working on eliminating them.

I'm walking, hiking, and exercising more, and I've reduced my intake of carbohydrates by at least 75 percent. These changes aren't only for the Thursday before the Friday-morning weigh-in. They're lifestyle choices that are becoming lifestyle changes.

Healthy lifestyle choices

Replace trigger foods. For me, it was chips and cookies. I've replaced them with seaweed snacks; my favorite is wasabi flavored. I also snack on edamame, almonds, and carrots. Another key for me is avoiding temptation; for example, I no longer walk down the cookie or chip aisles in the store. I stay away from the Friday-morning company doughnuts because I know I can't eat only one.

Sleep eight. Sleep at least eight hours a night. I've always believed I was a night owl and didn't need as much sleep as other people. The truth is, although I could function on less sleep, I wasn't at my optimum. It wasn't a healthy lifestyle choice. For me, the key was turning off the TV at night, not falling asleep with it on.

Smile and cry. Be happy. Be a glass-half-full person, and you'll live a longer, healthier, and happier life. But at the same time, don't hold it in when you need to let it out. A good cry is a healthy lifestyle choice. It not only gives relief, but, according to Dr. Judith Orloff, it also removes toxins. (Read "The Health Benefits of Tears" in *Psychology Today*.[24])

Stop stressing. Stress is a killer, mentally and physically. Research shows us that stress can lead to chronic illness, shortened lifespans, and mental duress.

Exercise. You don't have to run a marathon, bench 300 pounds, or do CrossFit seven days a week. You do need to get off the couch and exercise. My preferred activity is hiking because it accomplishes two things: exercise and time outdoors. For more of my thoughts on hiking (plus one of my favorite photos I've ever taken at Eagle Creek Park), read "The Health and Wellness Benefits of Hiking" at tkographix.com/the-health-and-wellness-benefits-of-hiking.

Your plan for improved health and wellness won't look like mine. Our needs, as well as our triggers and bad habits, aren't the same. However, like me, if want to change your life, you'll have to change your lifestyle.

---

[24] www.psychologytoday.com/blog/emotional-freedom/201007/the-health-benefits-tears

Chapter 8

Share Your Victories

Have you ever had one of *those* weeks at work? The kind of week where Murphy's Law was the rule: If it could go wrong, it did. I think most of us have experienced those days, weeks, and months. I once had a year like that until I figured out the workplace culture was no longer a match for me.

The answer to that situation was simple — I resigned. I didn't say it was *easy*; it wasn't. It was difficult. I had invested 10 years and helped the organization grow and prosper. However, whether it was the business that had changed or me, it was no longer rewarding, so it was a simple solution.

The point I want to make is that it's difficult to share your victories when it seems like there aren't any. However, that's not usually the case. There are usually victories to share if you look for them. They might be small, but they're still wins. And regardless of their scope, it's important to share your victories.

I have several people I share wins with. One co-worker and I take a few minutes every week and tell each other our recent victories. Once after telling me everything that was wrong with a recent conference, I asked what went right; she paused, thought, and then shared several positive takeaways from the conference. Later, she told me that considering what was good about the event refocused her on positive actions she could take.

We all have bad days

What if you enjoy your job but just had a bad day? The answer isn't quite as simple, but it's close. I love my job. Most days I arrive early. I often work from home on weekends because the inspiration hits me and I *want* to work, not because I feel obligated to do so. Does it get any better than that? However, as much as I love my job, it isn't perfect, nor am I. I still have those days and weeks where things just don't go as planned. So, here's what I do:

IDENTIFY WINS

Regardless of how bad things seem, there's always something that went right. Usually, there are victories to be found in any outcome, and if you're having trouble identifying a victory, turn your defeat into one. Use whatever went wrong as a lesson and map out how to avoid the defeat in the future.

CELEBRATE AND SHARE VICTORIES

I share wins with a friend. She tells me hers, and I talk about mine. Sometimes they're big, but not always. A win is a win, and regardless of its scope, it feels good to share. Every night when I get home, my wife asks about my day. It used to be that I'd tell her about my problems, but for the last few years, I've primarily shared what went right, not what went wrong. It's a lot more fun to share battles I've won rather than skirmishes I've lost.

You can't win 'em all

No, you can't win 'em all, but you can identify and share victories every day. If you look close enough, focus on the positive, and don't worry about the size of the win — you'll find your victories. And when you do and start concentrating on what you did well, your attitude and focus will reflect your successes. You have a choice: wallow in and eventually become defeated by your losses, or focus on your victories, learn from your defeats, and move forward. It's up to you.

Serving Others Promotes Action

Leadership is service. I heard those words for years but didn't really understood them until I found myself outside looking in. My title at TKO Graphix is Director of Communications — and we're still trying to figure out what that means. However, along with communication responsibilities, including blogs, video, and social media, I also, like many small to mid-size company employees, wear other hats. I'm privileged to work with several levels of employees on leadership training. I also have recruited, interviewed, and been part of the hiring process for quite a few of our employees. The thing is — I have zero direct reports. For the first time in 30 years, I "manage" no one … but I do *lead*.

Outside looking in, not being a manager, I believe I've become a better leader. Although I don't manage anyone directly, I have a vested interest in many of my teammates, and from this perspective, it's easier to see the most effective leaders are *leaders who serve.*

How do you move from being just a manager to being a leader who serves?

- **Set your ego aside.** Let's face it, if you're in a leadership role, part of why you became a manager is ego, but ego will often get in the way of effective leadership. Others are best served when ego is set aside.
- **Remind yourself that people are more important than projects.** When anyone oversees a project, it's natural to focus more on the plan than how the individual team members fit the plan, but success depends more on how team members execute the plan than the plan itself. Whether it's in the workplace, in a ballpark, or at home, try not to make people fit a plan; make a plan that fits them.
- **Help someone every day.** It's easy to get lost in the day-to-day battle and forget the big picture; the more you help members of your team, the more cohesive and loyal the team will grow.
- **Seek others' advice.** Once again, when you're putting out fires, it's easy to forget to seek input. By involving others in the plan, you may improve the plan and support of the plan. Make the team's plans, not your plans.
- **Share everything you know.** There should be little that is on a need-to-know basis; if it's useful, share it. Help others avoid mistakes, pitfalls, and problems. Teach others what has worked for you and what hasn't.

Service is not intangible. It's giving, caring, and sharing. If you care about people, there's no greater reward than watching others grow due, in part, to your influence. A true leader is not served — a true leader serves. Who have you served today?

Life

Giving Back

Chapter 9

Chapter 9: Giving Back

When it comes to giving back, too often I've had good intentions but didn't follow through with action. You can't talk charity done. I've learned that even for my volunteer and charitable contributions, I need a plan. Some plans are simple; for example, my wife and I contribute to charities in each other's name every Christmas.

For others I need a more detailed plan. For more than a decade, I've organized an annual blood drive in the summer and a toy drive over the holidays. Yesterday, I delivered 30 bags of presents, including seven bicycles, to our local Salvation Army headquarters for their Angel Tree Toy Drive. Without planning by myself and others, no presents, no bikes, would've been donated.

And then sometimes I'm called to give back in the most unlikely places, such as in line at a dollar store.

You Never Know When You'll Be Called to Give

I was shopping at my local Dollar Tree when I was handed an opportunity to give, to make a difference. If you're unfamiliar with Dollar Tree, everything in the store costs one dollar; it's the 21st-century version of the five and dime store. (Twice I've convinced cashiers to have some fun and announce over the store sound system, "Price check on register one." It's fun to watch folks in line stop and wonder.)

Anyway, I was in line when the register next to me closed. Two young ladies had been waiting longer, so I invited them to jump in front of me in line. It seemed the right thing to do.

Chapter 9

Both girls were wearing bright green camp T-shirts, which I asked about. They were camp counselors working at an Indy Parks camp for the summer. When I was a teenager, this camp was the local YMCA. I shared a few of my teenage memories with them.

I asked if it was a volunteer position or paid. They laughed and said paid, but not enough. They weren't being negative about it — just honest.

As I watched them empty their shopping basket, I noticed it was full of snacks — bags of unpopped popcorn, sunflower oil, pretzels, and cookies. I asked the young ladies who the snacks were for and was told it was for the kids at camp. It seems there wasn't much at the camp in the way of snacks.

And then I asked who was paying for it. I learned the girls were using their own money. I shared that both of my daughters had careers in education and had spent untold out-of-pocket dollars on school supplies.

As the cashier started to ring the two girls' purchases, I asked the cashier to please put their items on my tab. It was $22 — the best $22 I spent that week.

When I got home, I told my wife I had a present for her, and then handed her the receipt. She asked me what it was, and I told her the story. She put her arms around my neck, kissed my cheek, and said, "Thank you, it's a wonderful gift." Like I said, best $22 of the week.

Will you be ready when the opportunity to give presents itself?

Who Have You Helped Today?

Giving isn't about paying for the Starbucks of the person behind you in the drive-through. It's not about volunteering at a food bank or donating to the Salvation Army. And although all these efforts are thoughtful and commendable, it's really all about business networking.

Wait, what? What the heck does helping someone have to do with business networking?

I'm going to suggest a networking strategy that might seem counterintuitive. I want you to try this for one month, approximately 25 working days. Help someone every day for the sake of helping. Don't share an elevator pitch, discuss your needs, or ask for reciprocation — just help someone.

- **Help a co-worker.** When you take the time to get to know your teammates, understand their responsibilities, and comprehend their challenges, you begin building a better team. Asking how you can be of assistance and following through starts a process that will snowball. Not everyone will, but many will pay it forward, and some will pay it back to you.
- **Help a customer.** Not only with your product and service, but anywhere you can help them. For example, I've helped countless customers with guest blogs, social media advice, and video — not once asking for anything in return. But the return has come back to us tenfold. Folks remember who helped them.
- **Help a vendor.** Have you been part of a business–vendor relationship that became contentious? It happens much too often. Rather than combat each other over product, service, delivery, or price, wouldn't it make more sense to work together, to team up? Online retailer Zappos is a great example of this. Zappos made all its internal product and sales information available to vendors. Contrary to popular opinion, this didn't pit vendor against vendor but added 50+ members to the marketing team. The vendors used the information to improve merchandising. For the full story, read "Zappos Makes Nice with Vendors" at www.retailwire.com/discussion/15095/zappos-makes-nice-with-vendors.

There you have it. Help one person a day for the next 25 days without asking for anything in return. Help a teammate get their work completed. Help a customer find a client. Help a vendor by sharing information. Find someone to help every day. What have you got to lose besides a little time?

But let's say I'm wrong, and *your* teammates, customers, and vendors don't care if you help. You'll still feel good about what you've done.

Now go help somebody. Are you ready to take some action?

7 Ways a Small Business Can Give Back

Part of the culture at TKO Graphix is giving back. It's in our backbone. For more than 30 years, we've offered our help to the community and beyond. It's bonded our employees as teammates and strengthened our reputation. Besides, it feels good. Here are seven ways we give back that almost anyone can copy:

- **Pro bono work.** The legal term *pro bono* refers to "work undertaken for the public good without charge." At TKO, we've donated countless graphics. We've wrapped cars, semi-trailers, and even a motorcycle tank[25] at no charge to help a charity. And we've provided many others with our products at cost instead of at a profit. What product or service can you donate?
- **Sponsorships.** TKO sponsors events all year long. Occasionally, we're the lone benefactor, but more often we're an associate sponsor. Our contributions range from financial to donated products to offering a helping hand through volunteers.
- **Encouraging employee volunteerism.** At TKO, we have a committee that shares volunteer opportunities with our teammates. It ranges from helping at a pet shelter to creating bra art for a cancer fundraiser.
- **Leading by example.** The best example for us was the Angel Tree Toy Drive I mentioned earlier. TKO Graphix purchased a bike for every child who had a bike on their wish list. We added bikes to the gifts purchased by individual team members. We could almost see the smiles on the children's faces Christmas morning. And that's a pretty good example to set.
- **Supporting local organizations.** TKO Graphix sponsors local youth league baseball, softball, and soccer teams. The company also gives to local charities. One example of this is an annual Backpack Attack our volunteer team helps with, which is a school supply drive to benefit local schoolchildren in Hendricks County, the site of our main facility.
- **Spreading the word.** We do quite a bit with social media at TKO, and not a month goes by that we don't promote and support charitable initiatives. It only takes a moment and can make a difference.
- **Matching employees' contributions.** Learn what your employees are passionate about and offer to match their commitment.

Are you giving back enough? If not, why not? Here's a challenge for you: Choose one or two of the actions listed above and make them happen. Why? Because it will solidify your team and add to your standing in the community — and it just feels good. Now go make it happen!

---

[25] tkographix.com/miracle-ride-raffle-win-tank-bike

4 Steps to Donating Your Birthday

Last year I wrote a post called "Kyle's Challenge" about my teammate Kyle's participation in a TKO Graphix food drive.[26] The collection of canned goods and nonperishables benefited a local food pantry. When Kyle heard about the pantry and what TKO was doing, he donated his birthday to the food drive. It was his 35th birthday, and his parents had planned a party, but Kyle told them he wanted no cake or presents. He wanted gifts of food for the drive instead. He received more than 100 "presents" of foodstuffs. I was moved by what he had done and wondered what we could accomplish if more of us followed Kyle's lead.

How many presents and birthday cakes do you need? If you've had enough of both, it might be time to consider donating your birthday. It isn't terribly difficult.

Choose a charity. Do more than pick a charity you're familiar with; choose one you're passionate about. It could be a charity you already support with gifts, donations, or volunteer time. A good friend who is a military veteran donates his birthday every year to causes helping disabled veterans. It also may be a good idea to vet any charity before donating your birthday to it. Charity Navigator (www.charitynavigator.org) is a good place to start your research.

Issue a challenge. Set a goal. For example, Kyle had a goal of 100 pieces of food. He not only reached it but beat his goal, in part because he challenged his friends and family. Set a realistic goal, but one that stretches you, and then share it with your friends, family, and social media followers.

Share your goal. Kyle and his parents shared his goal in person and on the phone. It was the best way to reach them. Wherever your followers are is where you want to promote your call to action. Like Kyle, it could be best to reach out personally to your friends, or it could be better to post your call to action on Facebook or other social media.

It's simple to create a fundraising event on Facebook. On your home page, in the menu options to the left of your news feed, or under the menu in the upper right on the Facebook phone app, click "Fundraisers." (You might have to click "See More..." first.)

---

[26] tkographix.com/kyles-challenge

Facebook will give you all the information you need to set up and market your own fundraiser.

Tell a story. My friend who served in active duty has stories. He and his wife, who also served, don't talk about it a lot, but they have true tales. Their stories are moving, and when they do share their experiences, it's difficult not to join them in the support of the causes they've adopted. Would they be as successful in their charity campaigns if they didn't tell their stories? I don't think so. If you have a story behind the nonprofit you support — whether it's a time you volunteered and how it affected you or some other personal experience — share it.

But don't stop there. As the donation drive progresses, keep it updated. Share more stories and talk about what the charity can accomplish with the funds. Once you've established a goal, it's important to track and post progress toward your target.

Have You Heard of Giving Tuesday?

If you've heard of Giving Tuesday, that's wonderful. If you've participated in Giving Tuesday, even better. But don't feel alone if you're unfamiliar with it. According to *Philanthropy News*, although 93 percent of Americans know about Black Friday, only 18 percent are aware of Giving Tuesday. [27]

For many, the Thanksgiving holiday season has become one big shopping extravaganza. Black Friday, Small Business Saturday, and Cyber Monday have become as traditional as turkey, football, and the Macy's Thanksgiving Day parade. Don't get me wrong; I'm not disparaging this season of shopping. It's fun, most of the shopping is for gifts, and it's good for the economy. But shouldn't there be room for Giving Tuesday as well?

After the annual holiday stampede to the brick-and-mortar retail store or the online provider, shouldn't we all take a moment, a day, to share our gratitude by giving back? Is there a better way to show our thanks than by helping others?

What is Giving Tuesday?

---

[27] philanthropynewsdigest.org/news/18-percent-of-americans-familiar-with-giving-tuesday-survey-finds

Giving Tuesday began in 2012 as a response to the shopping frenzy the holiday has become. Founding sponsors Mashable, Skype, and Cisco enlisted other sponsors, such as Microsoft, and connected with charitable organizations to set the first Tuesday after Thanksgiving as a day of giving back. In 2016, *USA Today* reported that $168 million was donated on Giving Tuesday.

How to get involved
It's easy: give back. Support a local or national foundation with a donation. Volunteer at a shelter or food bank. Offer pro bono help, whether it's your professional expertise, a product you make, or a service you offer. Share your story and those of others on social media with the hashtag #GivingTuesday.

The Giving Tuesday website (givingtuesday.org) shares how individuals as well as organizations can get involved. "This November join the movement and give — whether it's some of your time, a donation, gift or the power of your voice in your local community. It's a simple idea. Whether you come together with your family, your community, your company or your organization, find a way to give back and then share your idea."

When Giving Back Comes Back

Do you believe in karma, in retributive justice? Do you subscribe to the belief that what goes around comes around? I do, but there's not always a direct link. In other words, just because you share an act of kindness with another human being doesn't mean they'll return the favor. People are people. Some are kind and considerate — others, not so much. But I've seen enough good things come back to those who have done good deeds, albeit not always directly, that I believe.

In life, in many ways, we get what we're looking for. I'm not talking about winning the lottery or marrying a movie star. I'm talking about what we think about, what we concentrate on, how we live our lives. We become what we believe, what we focus on. How we see the world becomes our reality, and that reality is what we find. For example, if you buy a brand-new blue model ABC car, suddenly you see new model ABC blue cars all over the place. Weren't they always there?

What you believe is what you'll find

Chapter 9

If you believe the world is full of anger and hatred, that's what you'll find. And if you think the world is full of good and grace, you'll find that as well. If in business you think everyone is out for themselves, then they are, and if you think most people are pretty good sorts and willing to help each other, that's what you'll find. Like I said, you'll find what you're looking for.

What's best for you?

Given a choice between, on the one hand, doing my best for others and feeling good about myself, or, on the other hand, allowing anger to live in my head, heart, and soul, I know I should choose the good, and I usually do. Doesn't it make sense that we as humans are healthier and happier when we look for the bright side and when we try to make a positive impact on others?

Yes, I believe in karma. Not in some mysterious spiritual way, but in that we control our karma. When we react in anger, we often receive anger in return. When we act with love and compassion, we may get it returned to us — not always, but often enough, at least for me, to make it worthwhile and meaningful. And besides, it feels good.

A story of karma

A co-worker and friend shared this story with me. Her morning routine is hectic (can you relate?): get the kids ready for school, feed the dog, pack lunches, be sure her fiancé is properly dressed — you know ... life in America.

After dropping the kids off at school, she had just enough time to grab a cup coffee for the morning commute and make a quick stop at the dollar store. As she pulled into the parking lot, she recognized a homeless man she'd seen before. So, she bought him a cup of coffee as well. When she went to give it to him, a homeless lady was by his side. She didn't have to think. She gave her cup of coffee to the lady. Without another thought, she quickly went to the dollar store.

In the store, an elderly man approached her and asked her name. At first, my friend was startled. She wondered why a stranger was following her. He told her he'd seen what she'd done with the coffee and asked why she didn't get herself a cup. She explained that she had but that she had given it to the lady and that in her mind it was no big deal. He said that he'd thought as much, and that it was a big deal. The man reached into his wallet and handed her a one-hundred-dollar bill, only saying, "This is for your kindness."

What's the lesson?

Is the lesson that when we do good, we'll be rewarded with hundred-dollar bills? No. Is it that we should do good in the hopes of a reward? Not really. Is it because that's what we're supposed to do? Kinda sorta.

The lesson is that when we do good things, it creates ripples. Like dropping a rock into a still pond, the ripple we create spreads in every direction. Some will reach other people, and they'll pass it forward, other ripples may hit the shore unimpeded, and still other waves may come back and wash over us. The lesson is, do good, and good will follow. If we all do enough good, it could create a tidal wave, couldn't it?

Volunteering Your Way to Better Health and Wellness

Volunteering is good for the soul and more. I assume everyone knows this, right? When I do good things, when I volunteer and help, I feel good. And when I feel good, it must mean good things are happening to me physically and mentally. Everyone knows this, don't they?

But wait, why are there so many angry people? Who are they helping with their rage? Don't they realize they may be damaging their well-being? Maybe everyone doesn't know that helping others is good for the body and soul. Do you?

How do you feel?

Are you one of the angry ones? At some level, you must know it's not good for you. Do you tell yourself volunteering would be great, but you just don't have the time? Several studies show that only 2 hours per week — 104 hours per year — of volunteering will reap huge benefits in health and wellness.

> A national survey of 3,351 adults conducted by Harris Interactive on behalf of UnitedHealth demonstrates that volunteering is good for your health. Here are some of the takeaways from this research: Volunteers say they feel better — physically, mentally and emotionally. —Eileen Cunniffe, "Study Underscores Health, Wellness and Career Benefits of Volunteering," *Nonprofit Quarterly*[28]

---

[28] nonprofitquarterly.org/2013/10/22/study-underscores-health-wellness-and-career-benefits-of-volunteering

Is your heart in the right place?
Seriously, those who give, who have their heart in the right place, experience improved health — even from heart disease. What ails you? Could volunteering be part of the answer for your health and wellness improvement plan?

> Using health and volunteering data from the U.S. Census Bureau and the Center for Disease Control, we find that states with a high volunteer rate also have lower rates of mortality and incidences of heart disease. — Robert Grimm Jr., Kimberly Spring, Nathan Dietz, "The Health Benefits of Volunteering," Corporation for National & Community Service[29]

Can you feel the pain?
Both the pain of those in need, and physical pain. Recent studies have shown that volunteering can improve the plight of chronic pain sufferers.

> People with chronic pain experienced a reduction in pain intensity and less disability when they started to work as peer volunteers for others suffering from chronic pain. —Rush University Medical Center[30]

It *is* better to give than to receive!
That giving is better than receiving isn't only a wise adage — it's the truth. Several studies have shown that those who give receive more than they share. They get happiness in return, and happiness is healthy.

> In one study, participants were asked to spend $5 on themselves or $5 on someone else. Guess which group was measurably happier? Those who spent money on other people! —Happify[31]

Make time to help
Not only can you find the time, but you should, and you should do it for yourself, for your health and well-being both physically and emotionally. Two hours per week is all it takes. Find a cause or charity that speaks to you, that moves you, and then make yourself available to help. It's not complicated. In return, you'll receive the benefits of happiness: improved health and mental well-being.

---

[29] www.nationalservice.gov/pdf/07_0506_hbr.pdf
[30] www.rush.edu/health-wellness/discover-health/health-benefits-volunteering
[31] www.happify.com/hd/science-of-giving-infographic

More ways to promote giving back
Here are a few more ways I've successfully promoted charitable actions. I've used some of these to increase awareness of a charitable initiative, others to enlist volunteers, and still others to seek donations.

- **Twitter chats.** Last week during a Twitter chat (#DigiBlogChat, Tuesdays at 4:00 p.m. EST), one of the regulars tweeted, "I wish there were more groups trying to solve a problem for the greater good. Think of the brilliance in this group — what we could create/change/solve. It's pretty amazing to think about." She went on to bring up the idea of supporting a charity as a group. We haven't moved forward yet, but this chat is full of smart, funny people who care and want to help. It's only a matter of time.
- **Networking groups.** I belong to a networking group that meets once a month to brainstorm ideas to help each other. That's it; we don't sell products or overly promote our businesses. We help each other. We've adopted, supported, and promoted dozens of charities, and the truth is, we could do more because, like #DigiBlogChat, this group cares.
- **Create a volunteer network.** If you enjoy giving back, why not form a group that shares and helps each other with charitable initiatives. Don't make this complicated. Invite a few people who have similar interests and needs. If you're a diabetic (as I am), invite other diabetics, or if you own a small business, invite small business owners. Are you an amateur photographer, chef, or horticulturist? Keep it simple. If you'd like to read more on this topic check out "Why Creating a Networking Group Rocks" at tkographix.com/creating-networking-group-rocks.
- **Taking action.** Mark Light took it into his own hands to promote his friends Chris and Liz Theisen. Their daughter, Emme, has faced physical challenges since she was a toddler. At the tender age of 5, she continues to fight the battle and has earned the nickname "The Princess Warrior." Mark created a fund and then rode a bicycle cross-country to bring awareness to her needs. If that isn't commitment, I don't know what a commitment is.

> Emme's medical expenses have strained the family's finances. Mark Light, co-founder of the Pancreatitis Foundation, did a cross-country bike ride that raised about $30,000 to help support the Theisens. But their overall costs run much higher even though the family has insurance. If you want to help,

Chapter 9

you can donate here at emmejo.com/donations. —Shari Rudavsky, "Meet Little Emme, Princess Warrior Battling Her Pain," IndyStar.com[32].

Conducting a Leaderless Group Exercise

Next, I want to share a fun experience I had working with a leadership group. In less than an hour, this exercise can teach any team how to work more productively, and like with many of the best lessons, they learn on their own.

Every Wednesday, I'm privileged to work with the TKO Graphix production department team leaders. These are entry-level supervisory positions, and for most of the leaders, it's their first management experience. The Wednesday before last Thanksgiving, we had an unusual, fun, and effective outing. I conducted a "leaderless" group exercise. The group was given a task, time limit, and conditions, but no instructions. It was their responsibility to devise a plan of action. The purpose was to show the importance of cooperation, compromise, and encouragement in a team dynamic.

The task was simple

We drove the group to a local discount store and given cash and a time limit to buy 20 toys that were to be donated to the Indiana Salvation Army's Christmas Assistance Angel Tree Toy Drive.

The group immediately began discussing how to divide the work. One of the managers took the lead by asking others their thoughts and ideas. For example, after deciding to allocate the shopping, she asked who would like to shop for boys or girls. They shared the amount each could spend, where each would go in the store, and then checked the remaining time. The assignment was successfully completed ahead of schedule. They learned the importance of planning, organization, and delegation, and how teamwork enhanced the process.

5 steps to a leaderless group exercise

- **Assign a simple task to the group.** An old classic involved erecting a tent without instructions. It could include assembling, creating, building, writing, or, like the example above, shopping. Be creative.

---

[32] www.indystar.com/story/life/2017/01/28/meet-little-emme-princess-warrior-battling-her-pain/96486068/

- **Set the stage** by explaining that all planning and activities will be up to the team.
- **Set conditions,** such as time limits and available resources.
- **Observe, but don't participate.** Believe me, you'll want to help, but the team will learn more without outside direction.
- **Review the results with the team.** What did they learn? How can the lessons be applied to the workplace?

Our team saw firsthand the effectiveness of cooperative team work. To them, it was the natural way to get the job done. The most important takeaway was when they realized they didn't always use these same leadership skills at the workplace. Conducting a leaderless group exercise can show how helping each other helps everyone.

4 Ways Corporate Giving Helps Your Business

Does your corporation give back to the community? Are employees involved in corporate giving? If so, you've already seen benefits from giving back, but there may be more reasons to participate in charitable giving than meets the eye.

Reduces turnover and increases productivity

One way to reduce turnover and increase productivity is employee engagement. While business leadership struggles for ways to engage employees, they often overlook corporate-sponsored volunteerism and giving. Organizations that help their employees give back have learned the benefits of bringing their team together in charitable engagement.

> Employees most committed to their organizations put in 57% more effort on their job — and are 87% less likely to resign than employees who consider themselves disengaged. —Shannon Schuyler, Nik Shah, Jeff Senne, and Clinton A. Moloney, "The Keys to Corporate Responsibility Employee Engagement," PWC.com[33]

Breaks down silos

Every organization develops silos where the part becomes greater than the whole. When an individual or department "silos," they withhold information from other departments and focus solely on their departmental needs, not on the needs of the organization.

---

[33] www.pwc.com/us/en/about-us/corporate-responsibility/assets/pwc-employee-engagement.pdf

(There's more in my post "Tear Down Your Silos!" at tkographix.com/tear-down-your-silos.) The way to tear down silos is for employees to interact, to get to know each other across divisional and departmental lines. One way to do this is through cross-training. Another method to break down walls and foster camaraderie is through volunteerism and charitable giving. Participation brings together team members from every position in every department.

Adds to corporate culture
Giving back not only influences corporate culture, it can help define it. An organization that is known for charitable initiatives is more attractive to prospective employees and potential customers. Being known as a company who cares goes beyond charitable giving because it informs clients that this same provider will care about their product and service. For employment recruits, a company that cares about responsible community involvement sends the message that they will surely care about employees.

Builds recognition
I don't want this to sound crass and commercial, but the truth is that charitable initiatives are a form of marketing. It's a way to focus media on a corporation. Whether it's branded signage at a local charitable golf outing or a spot on *Live at 5*, charitable actions shed a positive light on an organization.

There's another point of consideration about recognition: Volunteerism is a great way to recognize employees as well.

Is Your Corporate Giving Enough?

It would be difficult to find a business that didn't participate in corporate giving, but is it enough, and are employees involved? Ask yourself this: Does my organization's charitable giving involve all employees, add to our culture, bust silos, and improve productivity? If not, it may be time to reevaluate your corporate giving philosophy.

A Few Last Words

You can't talk shit done. However, you can turn any talk into an action planning vehicle. Don't be the leader who conducts a meeting with no action taken. And don't sit through one more meeting without finding a takeaway to act upon; regardless of whether the meeting facilitator issued a call to action or not, create your own action. Come to conferences prepared by knowing what you want to gain or who you want to meet, and then commit to acting. Do all this with every type of talk, including training, presentations, and seminars. Add action to your words in business and life and make giving back a recurring action.

Will moving from talk to action be easy? Not always. Does this little book cover everything you need to know about adding action to your words in every situation? Not even close. However, if you embrace the mindset of adding action to words, if you believe you can't talk shit done, and then you do your best to answer the call, it will make an impact.

It did for me. I talked about this book for a few months before I realized talking about it wasn't accomplishing much. I took action, and its results are in your hands.

So, let me ask you, what have you been talking about? Is it time to quit talking shit and get started? What's your plan of action?

Thank you,

Randy
Phone: 317-306-9713
Email: rclark@tkographix.com

Before I sign off, I want to leave you with one last *ACTION PLAN*. It's generic to a fault. It can be used for nearly anything you'd like to make better. If you're like me, you know the areas in your life and work that need improvement. So, don't talk about it; do something.

Improvement ACTION PLAN

Name _____

Date _____

Area of Improvement

_____
_____
_____
_____
_____
_____

Action Plans

What actions will be taken?

_____
_____
_____
_____

Who will be involved?

How will progress be monitored?

What worked?

_____
_____

What didn't work?

_____
_____
_____
_____

What was learned?

_____
_____
_____
_____

Acknowledgements

I want to acknowledge those who inspired me and taught me what I know about taking action, and those who helped me with this labor of love.

Madeline Kiley created the wonderful graphics for this book. I don't know what I'd do without the help of Nancy Jarial and the TKO Graphix design team. They rock.

Andy Hollandbeck won the honor of editing and formatting this book. It's the fourth book of mine that he's worked his magic on. He brings a wealth of knowledge and adds a level professionalism that without his help I couldn't reach.

My best friend, my wife Cathi, helped me in more ways than I can list. Cathi has spent more than 20 years giving back full-time. Twenty years ago, she walked away from a successful business career and dedicated her life to becoming a better human being and helping others. She has given back by taking action more than anyone I know.

Thank you all.

About the Author

Randy Clark is Director of Communications at TKO Graphix, where he blogs. Randy is passionate about social media, leadership development, and networking. He's the proud father of two educators, four amazing grandchildren, and a public-speaking wife. He lives in Speedway, Indiana, and on weekends he can be found performing rock 'n' roll with the Under the Radar band, running a 5K, flower gardening, or sharing an IPA.

From the Author

If I can answer any questions or assist you in any way, don't hesitate to reach out to me.

I work with organizations conducting leadership training. If you're interested in my help, let me know. I like to help, but I have three criteria I consider before taking an assignment: I believe in what the organization stands for, I know I can help, and it looks like fun.

If you have any questions, contact me at randyclarkleadership.com/#contact.

www.ingramcontent.com/pod-product-compliance
Lightning Source LLC
Chambersburg PA
CBHW081430220526
45466CB00008B/2327